FIELD GUIDE TO

BACKYARD BIRDS OF THE

WEST

Published by Cool Springs Press
A Waynick Book Group Company
101 Forrest Crossing Boulevard
Suite 100
Franklin, Tennessee 37064
(615) 277–5555

ISBN-13: 978-1-59186-009-9

First Printing 2008
Printed in the United States of America
10 9 8 7 6 5

Project Manager: Ashley Hubert
Art Director: Marc Pewitt
Production: Publication Services, Inc.
Illustrator: Publication Services, Inc.

Photographs of the American Tree Sparrow, American Woodcock, and Western Screech Owl courtesy of Jupiter Images. All other photographs provided by Brian E. Small.

FIELD GUIDE TO

BACKYARD BIRDS OF THE

WEST

COOL
SPRINGS
PRESS

FRANKLIN, TENNESSEE

CONTENTS

Introduction 8

Birds by color

INTRODUCTION

The dramatic landscapes of the West give rise to a number of fascinating species with unique adaptations. The brown-headed cowbird and western meadowlark make their home on flat grassland prairies where water is scarce. The mountain chickadee prefers the spruce-covered slopes of the Rocky Mountains. In temperate rainforests of the Northwest, the black phoebe and the hermit thrush dwell among some of the world's tallest trees. And in the four distinct deserts of the Southwest, curve-billed thrashers nest in saguaro cacti.

Although the West boasts a wide array of ecological zones, many bird species are unique to this half of the continent, separated from their eastern relatives by the Great Plains and the Rocky Mountains. As trees and gardens have been planted across the central grasslands, however, several species have crossed these traditional geographic boundaries to expand their ranges eastward.

If you are new to birding, a few basic strategies will increase the likelihood of spotting and identifying local species. The first step is to obtain at least one useful field guide. Carry it with you in the field, and keep it on hand for easy use. When you sight an unfamiliar bird, watch its behavior, note its coloring and unique field marks, and then consult your guide to confirm its name.

The second item to keep handy near your observation window is a pair of binoculars. A quality pair can often be purchased for under $100, and 7x or 8x magnification is ideal.

Learning to recognize bird songs is another valuable investment. Audio CDs and online resources provide samples of hundreds of common bird calls and songs, and knowing the sounds of your common backyard residents will make it easier to recognize an uncommon visitor.

Consider joining a local birding club. These organizations frequently organize birding walks and field trips, where more experienced birders can answer your questions, help you identify unfamiliar species, and recommend the best local bird-watching sites.

The simplest way to begin birding is to watch the birds in your own backyard. Even a small yard with one or two feeders can be home to dozens of birds. Some affordable options for seed-eaters include black-oil sunflower seeds, white millet, peanuts, mixed seed, cracked corn, and thistle seed. Insectivores may be hap-

California Towhee

pily at home among garden trees and shrubbery, but in winter, many turn to berries and suet cakes. Still others—hummingbirds, for example—are drawn to flowering plants.

Learning the dietary preferences of your favorite species can help you decide how best to draw them to your property. Bird boxes for cavity-nesting species are another easy way to intimately observe their behavior. Whether you encounter feathered friends close to home or far afield, birding is sure to become an exciting and rewarding hobby.

Anna's Hummingbird

red

T he commonly heard high-pitched, wiry warble of this sprightly hummer is noteworthy as the only North American hummingbird that sings to attract mates. But Anna's also uses a display flight that includes swooping dives from high in the air.

Description
The male is easily identified by his iridescent red crown, face, and throat patch. The female is slightly larger than female black-chinned and Costa's hummingbirds, with streaks of red on her throat. Both are stocky, only 3–4 inches long.

Preferred Habitat
Look for these flashy birds in scrub, open woods, suburban parks, and gardens. Their tiny, lichen-coated nests are built on a small branch or utility wire.

Feeding Habits
Using its long, needle-like beak, the hummingbird extracts nectar and small insects from flowers.

Migration Habits
Unusual among hummingbirds, most of these birds remain in their breeding range year-round, along the Pacific Coast from Washington to Texas. Their breeding range recently expanded into southern Arizona with the planting of flowering trees.

Placement of Feeders
Tubular red flowers featured in your garden are sure to draw Anna's and other hummingbirds, or plastic hummer feeders, serving up one-part sugar solution to four-parts water, are another low-cost lure.

RANGE MAP

LEGEND
- ■ Summer
- ■ Winter
- ■ Year-round
- ■ Migration

I n 1940 New York City pet shops began to sell California's native house finches as pet songbirds. In the ensuing crackdown on this practice, a small population of the brightly plumed birds was released.

red

Description
Similar to the purple finch of the North and West, the 6-inch male is brown above with a red brow, bib, and rump. The female, identified by a white eyebrow, and juvenile are paler with streaked bellies.

Preferred Habitat
Now widespread and common in both the East and the West, the house finch competes with the house sparrow for nesting sites and food in cities, towns, and farming areas.

Feeding Habits
Finches are common visitors to backyard seed feeding stations, and otherwise survive on fruit, bread crumbs, berries, buds, and flower parts.

Migration Habits
The introduced eastern population has thrived and spread across the continent, now separated from the native western population by less than 100 miles.

Placement of Feeders
While these welcome visitors are perched on your mixed seed feeder, try to distinguish the female house finch from the female house sparrow. Also, watch for finch nests in your hanging flower baskets or ornamental garden trees.

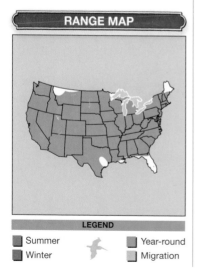

RANGE MAP

LEGEND

Summer	Year-round
Winter	Migration

Pine Grosbeak

A lthough less common than the pine siskin, the tame and approachable pine grosbeak is the largest finch of the North, where it is often seen eating small grains of sand to aid in digestion, or bathing in fluffy fresh snow.

Description
This large, stubby finch measures 8–10 inches, with a curved bill. The rosy male has dark streaks on his back, dark wings with two white bars, and a long notched tail. The female has a gray body with a dull yellow head and rump.

Preferred Habitat
During nesting season brushy clearings in coniferous forests are preferred, but deciduous forests provide a substantial portion of the bird's seed diet.

Feeding Habits
Regular travel is required as the grosbeak harvests the seeds and fruit of mountain ash and cedar trees. Insects supplement its diet in summer.

Migration Habits
Wintering south to the Dakotas and New York, these northern birds breed from Alaska across central Canada and south to California and Arizona.

Placement of Feeders
Although migrant populations vary from year to year, grosbeaks are occasional backyard visitors during migration. Distinguish the female from female purple finches or house finches by her large size.

RANGE MAP

LEGEND

Summer	Year-round
Winter	Migration

Only at close range can an observant birder distinguish the crossed bill tips of this tame species, specially adapted to pry open pine cones, releasing the seeds within. These nomads follow the pine cone crop, making them irregular backyard visitors.

Description
Breeding males are dull red above with black wings and tail, while nonbreeding males and females are yellow-green above and paler below. Adults measure 5-8 inches with a short, notched tail.

Preferred Habitat
Even hairless crossbill chicks in the nest consume conifer seeds, so unlike most birds, this species can reproduce at any time of year when there is a sufficient food supply. Females build a nest of plant fibers and pine needles in a coniferous tree.

Feeding Habits
Crossbills are entirely dependent on the seeds of spruce, pine, Douglas fir, and hemlock trees. Availability of this crop determines their migration habits and life cycles.

Migration Habits
These birds roam from southern Alaska across to New England and south through the Rockies and Appalachians. In winter, flocks follow the food supply, but most remain in the continental United States.

Placement of Feeders
Although unpredictable, crossbills may visit feeders for sunflower seeds or thistles. You may also see them at salt blocks or along salty roads.

RANGE MAP

LEGEND

■ Summer
■ Winter
■ Year-round
■ Migration

Red-winged Blackbird

From his perch on a swaying cattail, the male blackbird sings his gurgled song while flashing his red shoulder patches, eagerly establishing his mating territory before the females arrive.

Description
This large blackbird, 7–9.5 inches, is common and unmistakable. The black male has bright red patches on the shoulders, bordered by a yellow band. Females and juveniles are heavily streaked with brown and lack the red patches.

Preferred Habitat
Perhaps most common in marshes, swamps, and wet meadows, this marsh bird will nest near any body of water, including dry pastures, farmland, and roadside ditches. Breeding birds construct a new nest of marsh reeds for each of the season's two or three broods.

Feeding Habits
Seeds provide the blackbird's main sustenance in spring and autumn, but it switches to insects for the summer season.

Migration Habits
Their extensive breeding range stretches from Alaska across Canada and the United States, and the birds winter across most of the United States, north to Washington, Michigan, and Pennsylvania.

Placement of Feeders
The flashy red-wing is a familiar sight in backyards and parks across the country, particularly when they join up with other blackbirds for autumn and winter feeding in mobs of hundreds of thousands or even millions.

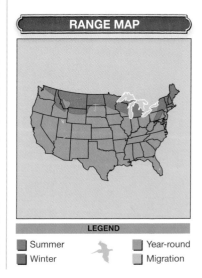

RANGE MAP

LEGEND

■ Summer   ■ Year-round
■ Winter   ■ Migration

S mall as a hummingbird and drably attired, the ruby-crowned kinglet is easily overlooked most of the year. But during spring mating, chattering males raise a concealed crown of red crest feathers—a "flash patch"—to challenge other males.

Description
The tiny, olive-green kinglet is whitish below with two white wing bars, a white eye ring, and a solid olive face. The male's red crown patch is usually hidden.

Preferred Habitat
Tiny nests constructed of moss and spider webs and decorated with lichen hang from twigs in a tall conifer. Coniferous forests are ideal for breeding, but they spread to mixed forests and thickets in winter.

red

Feeding Habits
Flicking its wings nervously in typical kinglet fashion, the bird bounds from branch to branch snatching aphids, spiders, and berries.

Migration Habits
Forests across much of the West are the kinglet's home in summer, and it is often glimpsed singing its surprisingly loud triplet song during migration. They winter across much of the southern half of the United States and West Coast, but can be found year-round in the far Northwest.

Placement of Feeders
Kinglets join up with mixed flocks of chickadees and warblers for winter foraging. Watch for a tiny bird fluttering around a thick shrub near the ground.

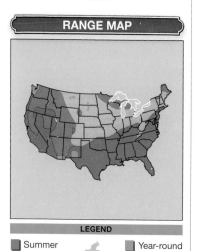

RANGE MAP

LEGEND

■ Summer
■ Winter
■ Year-round
■ Migration

American Bittern

brown

This master of disguise is so well camouflaged that birders may walk right past without noticing him. Sitting silently with its bill turned straight up to the sky, the bittern can take on the appearance of a tree stump, a root, or a dead limb, or it can sway back and forth to blend in perfectly with its reedy home.

Description

The pear-shaped bittern ranges from 24–34 inches long, streaked dark brown above, with dark wingtips and yellow legs and feet. Its white throat has long, reddish brown stripes.

Preferred Habitat

In secretive, isolated pairs the bitterns build a reed platform nest near the water's edge in marshes, fens, grassy lakeshores, large wetlands, or wet meadows.

Feeding Habits

Standing in the shallow water, the bittern waits in perfect stillness until a hapless fish draws near, then it plunges its stiff beak into the water to stab its meal. Insects, frogs, crayfish, reptiles, eels, and water snakes are common prey.

Migration Habits

This water-loving bird breeds throughout the northern half of the United States but can be found year-round along the Pacific Northwest coastline.

Placement of Feeders

In March and April, the usually solitary, silent males make brief public courtship displays. Between dusk and midnight, listen for a low-pitched *oonk-a-lunk* call.

RANGE MAP

LEGEND

■ Summer ■ Year-round
■ Winter ■ Migration

Only an experienced or diligent birder can distinguish the ash-coated from its close relatives the great-crested, brown-crested, and dusky-capped flycatchers. But listen for its distinct *ka-wheer* and *pic* calls.

Description
A medium-sized flycatcher at 8.5 inches, the bird is pale gray-brown above with a bushy crest and gray to yellow below. The wings and tail are marked with bright orange-red highlights.

Preferred Habitat
Unusual among flycatchers, this bird nests in cavities, often abandoned wood-pecker holes or natural crevices, but they may even evict a smaller bird from an occupied nesting site. The nests are lined with rabbit fur, hair, and shed snake skins. The species is common in arid, open groves, brushy fields, streamside thickets, and riparian forests of the West.

Feeding Habits
The flycatcher's main diet is insects gleaned from foliage or by flycatching, but it occasionally consumes fruit or small reptiles and mammals.

Migration Habits
From central Washington east to Colorado and south to Mexico this bird of the West breeds in summer, wintering in the southern part of its range. But every year, wandering migrants also turn up on the East Coast.

Placement of Feeders
This cavity-nester readily occupies man-made objects such as fence posts, mailboxes, pipes, or house eaves.

RANGE MAP

LEGEND

Summer
Winter
Year-round
Migration

brown

Bewick's Wren

brown

L oss of habitat, paired with the expansion of competing species, such as the house wren, house sparrow, and Carolina wren, have drastically reduced populations in the East, but Bewick's wren is still a common sight in the West.

Description
This backyard friend is brown above, white below, with a white eyebrow swash, measuring 5.5 inches long. It has a loud, melodious song, and its alarm call is *dzeeeb* or *knee-deep*.

Preferred Habitat
Favoring open fields or clearings with low-growing brush or thickets, Bewick's wren is often sighted in suburban backyards, especially near brush piles. They build nests at the base of trees or in man-made containers, such as baskets or sheds.

Feeding Habits
Spiders are a favorite delicacy for this insectivore.

Migration Habits
The relatively mild winters in its southwestern and southcentral range allow this wren to stay in place year-round, giving it an advantage over other competing migrant species such as the house wren.

Placement of Feeders
An alert and curious species, Bewick's wren is a happy cohabitant of human environments. If you spot one, try making a squeaking noise to incite its interest. It will respond with a distinct "irritation buzz" sound.

RANGE MAP

LEGEND

■ Summer
■ Winter
■ Year-round
■ Migration

Brown-headed Cowbird

Just before dawn, while a female songbird is away from her nest, an intruder rolls an egg out of the nest and replaces it with her own. The imposter fledgling will dominate the other chicks until it grows to maturity and rejoins its original species, the brown-headed cowbird. Often vilified as a brood parasite, the female cowbird leaves more than 20 eggs each season in the nests of more than 200 other species.

Description

The 6–8 inch glossy black male has a brown head, while the female is gray-ish brown overall. Both issue a *check* or rattling call.

Preferred Habitat

Once found only in the Great Plains, where it followed roaming buffalo

herds, the brown-headed cowbird has thrived on suburbanization and is today found from coast to coast, favoring woodland edges, thickets, roadsides, and towns.

Feeding Habits

Alongside other blackbirds and starlings, the cowbird forages on the ground for insects, seeds, and grains. Grasshoppers are a particular favorite.

Migration Habits

Migrating throughout the western United States in summer, these birds are found year-round in the Northeast, Midwest, and along the entire West Coast.

Placement of Feeders

This bird is drawn to grains, seeds, berries, cracked corn, or sunflower hearts.

RANGE MAP

LEGEND

- Summer
- Winter
- Year-round
- Migration

brown

a depression in the ground, sharing parenting duties with others in the colony.

Feeding Habits

Small "coveys" of these ground dwellers can be seen scratching the ground in open areas for seeds, acorns, flowers, leaves, berries, buds, and some insects. During long dry spells, they seek freshwater for drinking.

Migration Habits

These natives of the West reside year-round from Washington to southern California, and east into Nevada and Utah.

Placement of Feeders

Quail are tolerant of humans and will graze on cracked corn or millet spread on the ground. Listen for their loud *coo-ca-cow* calls.

Social and gregarious, these plump little birds are easily recognized by the dark feathery plume springing straight from their foreheads. Beloved as the state bird of California, the quail is also a favorite among game hunters.

Description

The 11-inch adults are blue-gray above with brownish wings, a gray breast, white-striped gray flanks, and a scaly-patterned white belly. Males have a brown crown and black face, with a bold white eyebrow and white "necklace." Females have a brown head and face.

Preferred Habitat

A variety of habitats host this species, including open brushy areas, canyons, chaparral, and residential areas. Nesting in communal broods, adults lay eggs in

RANGE MAP

LEGEND

■ Summer   ■ Year-round
■ Winter   ■ Migration

Towhee pairs mate for life and are aggressively committed to each other. If a pair is separated while foraging in flocks, at their next meeting the two reassert their bond with a brief dance and a loud, squealing duet.

Description
Large and unremarkable, this 10-inch sparrow is mainly dull brown above and below.

Preferred Habitat
In urban and rural California, the towhee resides in mixed woodlands, gardens, lawns, or fields, often in close proximity to humans. It constructs a bulky nest of twigs low in a tree or bush, where pairs raise two or three broods a year. Only the final brood of fledglings remains with their parents through autumn.

brown

Feeding Habits
Foraging on the ground in lawns, parking lots, and grassy areas, the bird consumes seeds, grain, and insects.

Migration Habits
This bird is found primarily in California and southern Oregon year-round. It was once classified with the canyon towhee under the name brown towhee, but they are now recognized as distinct species whose ranges do not overlap.

Placement of Feeders
Confirm the identity of the large brown bird hopping under your seed feeder with its long tail cocked by observing its rusty undertail coverts and its clanging *chink* call.

RANGE MAP

LEGEND

- Summer
- Winter
- Year-round
- Migration

Cedar Waxwing

These sleek, elegant birds are highly social, often seen lined up on a wire or branch passing berries or flower petals from one bird to the next. Best identified by a narrow, black "bandit" mask across the eyes, the crested bird has yellow tail tips and waxy red tips on the inner wing feathers.

Description
The 8-inch waxwing's plumage is a beautiful blend of soft pastel browns and grays above and below.

Preferred Habitat
Waxwings enjoy the close company of their own kind, making them one of the few songbirds to nest in colonies. They build bulky twig nests in open woodlands, orchards, gardens, and parks.

Feeding Habits
The bird consumes mainly berries and flower buds from berry-bearing trees and shrubs, especially cedar cones. Overripe, fermenting berries cause temporary intoxication, a startling sight for observant birders. During summer they also catch insects.

Migration Habits
This stunning species breeds across the northern half of the United States wintering in the lower United States from the East Coast to the West Coast.

Placement of Feeders
Announcing their arrival with a high-pitched whistling, small winter flocks frequently descend on parks and gardens in search of cedar and rowan berries.

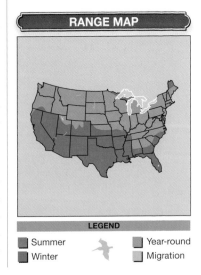

RANGE MAP

LEGEND
Summer
Winter
Year-round
Migration

Along the Pacific Coast only one chickadee is common, and this stout, colorful creature blends perfectly into the redwood and conifer forests of that region. Outgoing and spunky, an active chickadee's heart can beat up to 800 times a minute.

Description
As its name suggests, the 5-inch adult chickadee has a rust-brown back, a dark brown cap, a black bib, white cheeks, and rusty sides.

Preferred Habitat
This species favors the Pacific's widespread coniferous forests, parks, and gardens. Sometimes nesting in colonies, they construct a loose cup of plant fibers and moss in a natural or newly excavated tree cavity.

brown

Feeding Habits
As in all mixed flocks, competition for food is minimized as each species sticks to a certain foraging technique or specific foraging location. The chestnut-backed, like other acrobatic chickadees, gleans insects from foliage and consumes pine seeds and berries.

Migration Habits
From the great Pacific Northwest to Southern California, this bird can be found year-round. In late summer they join mixed flocks for winter foraging.

Placement of Feeders
Careful observation of winter mixed flocks can be the easiest way to spot this gregarious chickadee. At feeders their favorites include sunflower hearts, black-oil sunflower seeds, suet, and peanut butter.

RANGE MAP

LEGEND
- Summer
- Winter
- Year-round
- Migration

Chipping Sparrow

A bandoning its ground foraging for the moment, a male chipping sparrow mounts a high perch to utter its rapid, monotonous trill, often likened to the sound of a sewing machine.

Description
Six-inch adults are brown streaked with black above and gray on the rump, sides, and underparts. Look for its chestnut crown, white eyebrow, and black line through the eye.

Preferred Habitat
Often found in backyard shrubs or evergreens, the bird thrives in farmland, orchards, open woodlands, and residential areas. High in a tree, the female lines a cup nest with hair plucked from a horse or dog to insulate the season's two broods.

Feeding Habits
In summer the chippy eats primarily insects, including spiders, caterpillars, wasps, weevils, grasshoppers, and other agricultural pests. In autumn small flocks forage on lawns for grass and weeds, surviving on seeds in winter.

Migration Habits
Notable as the most common migrant sparrow in North America, this bird has a long breeding season throughout most of the United States, wintering along the Gulf Coast into the Desert Southwest.

Placement of Feeders
Any birder with access to a developed backyard garden is sure to enjoy the presence of the domesticated chippy as it scours the ground beneath feeding stations.

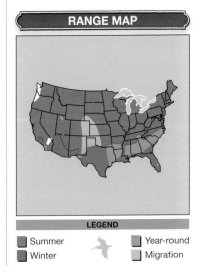

RANGE MAP

LEGEND
■ Summer
■ Winter
■ Year-round
■ Migration

brown

During spring migration, the otherwise elusive fox sparrow conspicuously spouts loud, melodious warblings from a shrub or thicket. This sparrow—a separate genus from other sparrows—has 18 different subspecies in North America.

Description

Western birds are brownish or slate-colored and red-striped. Eastern birds are fox colored with orange-red wings and tail and blue-gray highlights on the head. The Rockies version is gray above with a reddish tail, while sparrows of the Pacific Northwest are darker above with a slightly reddish tail. All measure approximately 7.5 inches.

Preferred Habitat

As a ground nester, the sparrow makes its home in dense woodland thickets, overgrown coniferous forests, or in grassy pastures or roadsides.

Feeding Habits

Equipped with unusually large feet and claws, the fox sparrow, like the eastern towhee, finds its meals by noisily double scratching among leaves for seeds, berries, or insects.

Migration Habits

Though most of its breeding range is found throughout the Rocky Mountain range, this sparrow winters in the Deep South and all along the West Coast.

Placement of Feeders

A smacking *tssk!* call or noisy scratching in leaves reveals the backyard presence of this shy visitor. Red cedars or elderberry bushes draw the sparrows in winter.

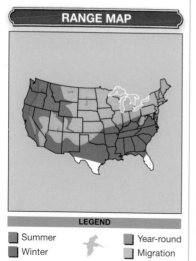

RANGE MAP

LEGEND

■ Summer
■ Winter
■ Year-round
■ Migration

The 7-inch sparrow of the Pacific Northwest demonstrates highly systematic behavior. For example, birds return to the same wintering grounds year after year, and at feeding stations each bird consistently visits a specific spot on the feeder.

Description

Named for their bright yellow crown patch, this large sparrow is slender and long-tailed. Breeding birds are streaky brown above and gray below, with a black cap and collar and two white bars on brown wings. Winter birds have a brown cap with a paler crown.

Preferred Habitat

For breeding season this species makes its home in alpine meadows and forest clearings, where mating pairs dig a shallow depression at the base of a tree for their nest. In winter the birds can be found in dense thickets or brushy fields.

Feeding Habits

With its two-tone bill, the sparrow consumes seeds and seedlings, buds, flowers, and some insects.

Migration Habits

This sparrow spends more time in its wintering grounds of coastal Washington, Oregon, and California than any other migrant species. It then heads into British Columbia and Alaska to breed.

Placement of Feeders

In its range the golden-crown is a common backyard visitor. Watch for its short, jerking flight and listen for a clear, three-note whistling call.

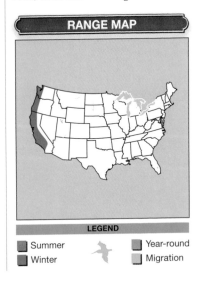

RANGE MAP

LEGEND

Summer

Winter

Year-round

Migration

A lovely, hymn-like fluting song at twilight has earned the hermit thrush much admiration. Its long, rolling notes vary in pitch and volume, making it difficult to pinpoint the songster.

Description

The 7.5-inch thrush is olive-brown above and boldly spotted buff below. The face is gray with a white eye ring, but the best field mark is its reddish tail.

Preferred Habitat

This forest bird can be found in coniferous or deciduous woodlands or wooded swamps, bogs, and fields. The female builds a well-concealed ground nest, and the male helpfully feeds his incubating mate.

Feeding Habits

In spring and summer the bird forages

brown

on the ground and gleans vegetation for ants, butterflies, bees, moths, and spiders. In winter they subsist on wild fruits, buds, and berries.

Migration Habits

If you spot a spotted thrush in winter, it must be the hermit thrush. This species winters across the southern United States, but as soon as beetles emerge in early spring, they head north into the Rocky Mountain range and along the Pacific Northwest Coast.

Placement of Feeders

Suet cakes, raw apples, pecans, and peanut butter may attract this woodland bird to a backyard feeder. Watch for its characteristic tail-bobbing; this is the only thrush to wag its tail.

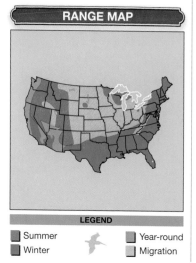

RANGE MAP

LEGEND

■ Summer

■ Winter

■ Year-round

■ Migration

Horned Lark

Of the world's 75 true lark species, the horned lark is the only one widespread in North America. The clearing of eastern forests made way for this bird of open spaces, which often makes its home on prairies, air fields, farmland, or Arctic tundra.

Description

Although its black "horns" are rarely visible, the 8-inch lark is very distinct with its black markings on the head and black crescent band across the breast. The face is white or yellow and the black tail is rimmed with white.

Preferred Habitat

In a spectacular courtship display, males soar to heights of up to 800 feet, then nose-dive silently back down. Their nests—in a shallow depression on the bare ground—are vulnerable to late storms or spring planting.

Feeding Habits

Walking slowly along the ground and scratching with its large feet, the horned lark searches for grain, seeds, insects, or spiders.

Migration Habits

This bird breeds all across the United States except in the Southeast; its yearly migration takes it to the West Coast.

Placement of Feeders

Larks gather in flocks of up to thousands in late autumn, often joining with longspurs and buntings. They may be seen along roadsides or croplands, often singing in flight.

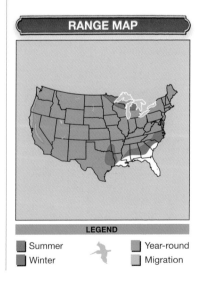

RANGE MAP

LEGEND

■ Summer ■ Year-round
■ Winter ■ Migration

In an effort to control crop pests, house sparrows were imported from England in 1850 and released all over the United States. They have since spread throughout the entire continent, where they thrive in human-altered environments (part of their Latin name is *domesticus*). Unfortunately, these aggressive competitors have diminished the success of native cavity nesters such as bluebirds and tree swallows.

brown

Description
Males, up to 6.5 inches long, have a gray crown and rump, black bib, white cheeks, and chestnut head stripes, while the female and young are streaky brown above and white below.

Preferred Habitat
Resourceful and friendly, the house sparrow is at home in cities, suburbs, and farmland, where it constructs nests of grass, feathers, and bits of rubbish in a man-made or natural cavity.

Feeding Habits
The sparrow squabbles fiercely over territory, mates, and food, the latter including insects, grains, berries, and weed seeds.

Migration Habits
Some birds of the past experienced involuntary migration, touring the country by rail while snacking on spilled grain in train cars, but the house sparrow has become an abundant permanent resident throughout North America.

Placement of Feeders
A familiar sight at every backyard feeder, house sparrows are drawn to bread crumbs, seeds, and grain.

RANGE MAP

LEGEND
Summer
Winter
Year-round
Migration

it nests in a shallow depression in the ground.

Feeding Habits

Like other plovers, killdeers feed with a stop-start action of chasing prey and standing still, then pecking in the dirt with their bills to seek seeds and insects, earthworms, and snails.

Migration Habits

As early as February, some killdeers migrate north to breed. However, they can be found from the East Coast to the West Coast throughout the year.

Placement of Feeders

Killdeers are common and easy to identify, but if you spot an adult male giving the broken-wing display, retreat and do not disturb them.

Nearly every vacant lot or golf course is home to this noisy plover. When threatened, the adult bird feigns injury, dragging its wing as if broken, to lure predators away from the nest. These shorebirds flee by sprinting along the ground or swimming to safety.

Description

Named for its shrill *kill-deer* alarm call, the species measures 9–11 inches, colored brown above and white below, with a rust-colored rump, long legs, and a black-and-white tipped tail. Adults have two identifying black bands across the chest, though chicks have only one.

Preferred Habitat

Any short-grassed open field, river bank, or gravel road edge with water nearby can house the killdeer, where

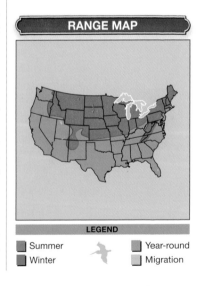

RANGE MAP

LEGEND

Summer   Year-round
Winter   Migration

The polygamous male builds up to 20 "dummy" nests to serve as courting sites for potential mates. Interested females then construct their own nests. This abundance of nests, most unused, makes it difficult for competing species to enact revenge when the marsh wren pierces the eggs of nearby wrens and larger blackbirds.

Description

Smaller than a sparrow at 4–5.5 inches, the wren is brown above, pale buff below, with a white-streaked back and white eyebrow. Males define and defend their territory with up to 200 different songs.

Preferred Habitat

The marsh wren prefers wetlands, particularly freshwater or brackish marshes with abundant cattails, bullrushes, or reeds. These plants are used to construct a nest attached to reeds.

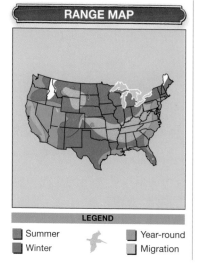

RANGE MAP

LEGEND

- ■ Summer
- ■ Winter
- ■ Year-round
- ■ Migration

Feeding Habits

This flycatcher consumes aphids, beetles, wasps, bees, mites, and larval dragonflies, and plucks other aquatic insects and snails from their marshy home.

Migration Habits

This bird has an extensive breeding range spanning the United States from north to south. It can be found year-round, however, only along the Atlantic and Gulf Coasts and in the far West.

Placement of Feeders

Patient observation in the bird's habitat may be rewarded with a brief glimpse of its cocked tail. Listen for the male's call, reminiscent of a mechanical sewing machine.

With 70 million shot annually, the mourning dove ranks as America's most popular game bird. The species boomed with the large-scale felling of forests, and its mournful *coo-ah, coo, coo* song is recognizable in all urban and suburban environments.

Description
This 12-inch sandy-colored dove has black wing spots and a long tapered tail bordered with white. Males are slightly brighter, with a pink sheen along the neck.

Preferred Habitat
The resilient mourning dove thrives from farmland to irrigated deserts, open fields, parks, and lawns. Their stick nests, built in tall trees, low bushes, or on the ground, are flimsy and poorly constructed, but home to at least two broods annually.

Feeding Habits
Like other doves and pigeons, this dove feeds its young regurgitated, protein-rich food known as "pigeon milk" produced in the adult's gullet. Birds may fly several miles at dawn or dusk in search of seeds, insects, or the nearest water source.

Migration Habits
Hundreds of birds may congregate for autumn migration from the southwest regions of Canada south throughout the continental United States.

Placement of Feeders
The backyard birder has only to listen for the dove's song to recognize this frequent feeder visitor. Watch for their fast silhouettes flying at early morning or dusk.

RANGE MAP

LEGEND

■ Summer ■ Year-round
■ Winter   ■ Migration

A loud, repeated *flicker* or *wick-wick-wick* ringing in the forest canopy announces the breeding season of this unusual woodpecker. Three color variations exist—yellow-shafted (East), red-shafted (West), and gilded (Southwest)—but they interbreed where their ranges overlap.

Description

Large at 10–14 inches, flickers are black or brown with tan bars above, with a pale spotted breast and bright underwings. Eastern birds have yellow under the wings, a red nape, and a black "mustache" on males. Western birds have red underwings, rump, and mustache. Southwestern varieties have yellow underwings and a red mustache.

Preferred Habitat

Spot the flicker in open country near large trees, such as farmlands, parks,

brown

woodlands, deserts, and suburbs. They nest in a tree cavity or burrow into fence posts, rafters, or even saguaro cacti.

Feeding Habits

Foraging on the ground, the flicker extends its enormous tongue to lap up ants. It also consumes insects, fruit, and seeds, occasionally flycatching.

Migration Habits

Although year-round residents of the United States, these birds migrate north for the breeding season and return south to winter in south Texas and in the Desert Southwest.

Placement of Feeders

Watch for these ground feeders eating ants and beetles on lawns or sidewalks. They may also visit suet feeders.

RANGE MAP

LEGEND

- Summer
- Winter
- Year-round
- Migration

brown

raising their young in a dead tree.

Feeding Habits

Clinging with long toes, the nuthatch creeps up and down tree trunks, foraging in pine cones for conifer seeds and insects, and using its strong beak to crack open seeds.

Migration Habits

When conifer seeds are sparse in northern states, these birds head south. They breed across Canada, but can be found year-round throughout the western United States.

Placement of Feeders

Though less common than its white-breasted relative, the red-breast will visit seed or suet feeders and use a birdhouse. Its nasally *yank-yank* call is higher pitched than the white-breast.

Nuthatches have an inexplicable habit of spreading layers of pine resin around the outside of the nesting cavity while they raise their young. The pitch sometimes smears on the adults' feathers, making them look messy.

Description

This small, stocky bird, only 5 inches long, is blue-gray above with a black crown (gray on females) and rusty red below. They are the only nuthatches with a white eyebrow and a black stripe through the eye.

Preferred Habitat

A preference for conifers makes these birds more numerous in the North and the West, but they expand their range during winter. Like all nuthatches, these birds nest in cavities, usually

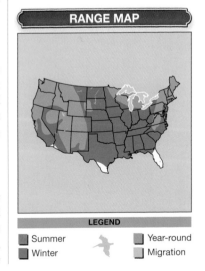

RANGE MAP

LEGEND

Summer   Year-round

Winter   Migration

Red-eyed Vireo

Continuous singing from the forest canopy allows birders to readily identify this vireo, the most abundant bird in Eastern deciduous forest.

Description
This small songbird, measuring 5 inches, is olive-brown above and whitish below. From the crown, identifying marks include its blue-gray cap, white eyebrow, and red iris.

Preferred Habitat
Vireos are common in deciduous and mixed forest, as well as urban and residential areas with mature trees. Females lay eggs in an open cup of twigs and bark suspended in forked branches. Unfortunately, this species is the most common victim of the brown-headed cowbird's nest parasitism.

Feeding Habits
Scooting along a branch, the vireo plucks a fat caterpillar with its foot, lifting it to its mouth one bite at a time. Insects comprise nearly 90 percent of its summer diet, but in winter most birds subsist on fruit.

Migration Habits
Singly and in pairs, vireos make an annual migration to their breeding range east of the Rockies and north into the Pacific Northwest.

Placement of Feeders
Watch for this persistent vocalist perched high in the treetops. The vireo's presence may be revealed by its song, a series of slurred phrases—*Here I am! See me, see me?*—separated by short pauses.

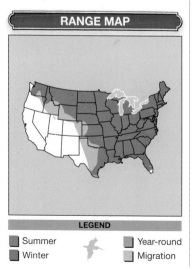

RANGE MAP

LEGEND

Summer

Winter

Year-round

Migration

brown

Savannah Sparrow

brown

Seventeen races of this species are recognized, varying in color and weight. These regional variations develop because most savannah sparrows return year after year to the area where they hatched.

Description

Plumages vary from pale brown to darker chestnut above and pale below. Most races, measuring 4–6 inches, have a pale stripe through the crown.

Preferred Habitat

The aptly named sparrow is found in large open spaces of short grass and weeds, from tundra to marshland to golf courses. Beneath a shrub or tuft of grass the female weaves a shallow nest of grass, often home to two broods each season. Males maintain several mates.

Feeding Habits

This sparrow is a ground dweller, running and hopping in search of grasshoppers, ants, and spiders. Insects make up most of the sparrow's diet in summer, while in winter they frequently roost among sorghum crops, a source of seeds through the cold months.

Migration Habits

Breeding grounds for this bird span the Pacific Northwest and across northern states. It winters across the southern third of the United States from the East to West Coasts.

Placement of Feeders

Identify this sparrow in your backyard by noting the bird's darkly streaked underparts, its short, notched tail, and the yellow spots in front of the eyes.

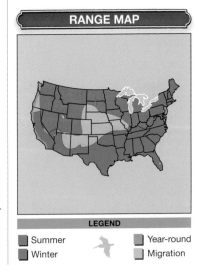

RANGE MAP

LEGEND

■ Summer ■ Year-round
■ Winter ■ Migration

From spring breeding season through autumn, and even into winter in the North, the aptly named song sparrow serenades his mate with more than 20 different songs, improvising more than 1,000 variations on these melodies.

Description

Coloring varies from rust to gray to streaked brown above, but all measure 5-7 inches long, with a brown eyebrow and a central spot in a streaked white breast. Juveniles lack the central breast spot and may be mistaken for the savannah sparrow.

Preferred Habitat

Song sparrows make their homes in thickets, gardens, parks, and roadsides, where they raise up to three broods each year. Fledglings begin to develop their own song repertoire before they

even leave the nest.

Feeding Habits

These ground feeders use their feet to rustle up insects, seeds, grain, and berries. In flight, watch the sparrow's characteristic pumping of its long, rounded tail.

Migration Habits

Traveling solo or in pairs, song sparrows are found throughout the United States year-round, but winter from the Deep South into the Desert Southwest.

Placement of Feeders

Although common and widespread in North America, a song sparrow at a backyard feeder is a rare occasion. But if you locate a nearby nesting pair, watch for them to return year after year.

RANGE MAP

LEGEND

Summer
Winter
Year-round
Migration

brown

Once known as the bay-winged bunting, this familiar farmland sparrow was renamed for its sweet serenade to the setting sun. This ground dweller alights on the highest available perch to sing its descending trill throughout the day, but it is the only sparrow to sing regularly at twilight.

Description

The 6.5-inch vesper sparrow is streaked gray-brown above and pale and streaked below. Its white-rimmed tail and orange-red shoulder patches are the best identifying field marks.

Preferred Habitat

This bird is one of only a handful of species common in prairies, fields, meadows, and roadsides in farm country. The nest is sunk into a shallow dent in the ground, leaving their broods vulnerable to the threat of early mowing or cultivation.

Feeding Habits

Running along the ground, the vesper sparrow halts to pick up grain, weed seeds, and insects. Its fondness for agricultural pests, such as weevils, make it a welcome addition to cultivated fields.

Migration Habits

The coastal states, from California to New England, are wintering grounds for these songsters, but breeding season is spent across the north half of the United States, with the greatest numbers in the West.

Placement of Feeders

Scatter cracked corn below your feeding stations to draw solo birds or mating pairs in winter and early spring.

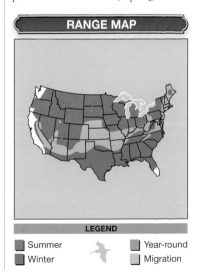

RANGE MAP

LEGEND

■ Summer
■ Winter
■ Year-round
■ Migration

This finch is commonly known as the wild canary for its appearance and song. As it hops along summer fields gleaning thistle seeds, the male bird's bright yellow and black plumage is unmistakable.

Description

The summer breeding male is easily recognized, with its lemon-yellow coloring, and black cap, wings, and tail. At 5 inches long, the female and winter male are significantly duller yellow with black wings and tail.

Preferred Habitat

Fields, groves, thickets, farmland, and weedy grasslands provide a steady supply of small insects and seeds year-round.

Feeding Habits

In spring, when insects are plentiful, they account for up to 50% of the goldfinch's diet. Seeds are its main staple through late summer and autumn, with berries supplementing in winter.

Migration Habits

Spring is ideal breeding time in western states, but in the East goldfinches commonly wait until late summer, when weed seeds are readily available. They travel in flocks of up to 20, but are hardy enough to winter across much of their normal range.

Placement of Feeders

Feeders offering nigel thistle seeds and sunflower seeds are sure to draw these birds to your yard, and they are frequent visitors during the winter months. The goldfinch also loves birdbaths.

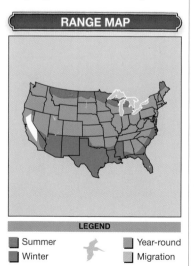

RANGE MAP

LEGEND

- Summer
- Winter
- Year-round
- Migration

yellow

Common Yellowthroat

O ften called the Maryland yellow-throat, where it was first collected in 1766, this sweet songbird is elusive and rarely seen. The male yellow-throat twitters from perch to perch, marking his territory and defending it aggressively.

Description
The small black-masked male issues a sharp *chek* call from his bright yellow throat. The 6-inch female, lacking the mask, responds with a gentle *wichity, wichity* song.

Preferred Habitat
Brushy swamps, wet thickets, or over-grown marshes, and tangles of weeds or berry bushes provide sufficient cover for the ground nests of these polyga-mous birds.

Feeding Habits
Hovering low over a clump of cattails, the yellowthroat scoops up adult and larval insects such as spiders or dragon-flies, supplementing its diet with seeds.

Migration Habits
Migrating from South and Central American into the entire United States during summer, this species is the northernmost yellowthroat in the west-ern hemisphere. Though not its usual habitat, the migrating birds may be found far from water.

Placement of Feeders
This shy but curious species can be roused from their tall-grass hideouts by various noises. Try making a squeaking noise by kissing the back of your thumb, give a low growl, or make a *psssh-psssh* sound.

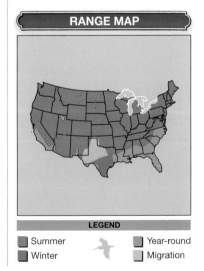

RANGE MAP

LEGEND

■ Summer	■ Year-round
■ Winter	■ Migration

yellow

Birders unfamiliar with this species might describe it as a huge American goldfinch. But note the large, powerful beaks for which they are named.

Description
Grosbeaks are stout and round with short tails. Males are olive brown above and yellowish below, while females are grayish above. Males are easily identified by the dark head, bright yellow forehead band, and white wing patches.

Preferred Habitat
Generally this bird lives in spruce and conifer forests, only venturing into residential areas for sunflower seeds. High in a conifer the female builds a loose, fragile nest of twigs and moss.

Feeding Habits
In summer this species consumes large

quantities of insects, but their conical bills are also well suited to cracking seeds and buds.

Migration Habits
The introduction of box elder and maple trees, as well as feeding stations, has drawn these birds eastward to the Atlantic. However, they can still be found year-round throughout the Rocky Mountain range into the Pacific Northwest.

Placement of Feeders
Flocks of friendly, social evening grosbeaks are easily lured to a backyard feeding station featuring sunflower seeds, where they may remain for a few hours or a few months. Their ringing *cleer* call sounds like a loud house sparrow.

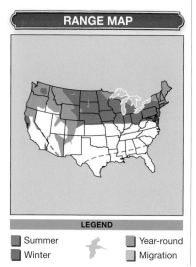

RANGE MAP

LEGEND

■ Summer ■ Year-round
■ Winter ■ Migration

yellow

Lesser Goldfinch

For centuries the lesser goldfinch was kept as a cage bird, the brilliantly plumed male singing its rapid, twittering song incessantly except during its molting period. Young males in their first breeding season are drab like the female, but seem to enjoy the same breeding success as the elaborately colored older males.

Description

This tiny bird, only 4 inches long, boasts a variety of male patterning, with backs from olive green to black and underparts from pale buff to bright yellow. Adults have black wings with white markings on the wings and tail. Females resemble the American goldfinch, but with a dark rump.

Preferred Habitat

Nesting in a bush or low tree, goldfinches are found in forests, savannas, gardens, or brushy country.

Feeding Habits

Dandelion seeds and thistle seeds are so central to the bird's diet that their breeding cycle adapts to the availability of this food source. The fledglings are fed soft, unripe dandelion seeds.

Migration Habits

The goldfinch is found north to Washington and northern Nevada and east to Colorado and Texas.

Placement of Feeders

Feeders featuring thistle seeds are a favorite with goldfinches, and an abundance of dandelions may draw them as well.

RANGE MAP

LEGEND

- Summer
- Winter
- Year-round
- Migration

In 1811, when Alexander Wilson discovered this warbler in Tennessee, the bird was not a common resident. But the clearing of vast forests generated the overgrown pasture favored by the Nashville warbler, now a common migrant throughout much of North America.

Description

This 5-inch warbler is olive above and bright yellow below, with a white patch on the belly between the legs. The male's pearly gray head has a white eye ring and a usually concealed red crown patch. Females have an olive-colored head and a blue-gray neck.

Preferred Habitat

During migration the warbler can be found in woodlands, shrubs, and suburbs, while it breeds in brushy fields, young woodlands, and groves. Its ground

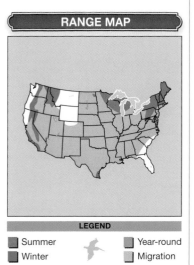

RANGE MAP

LEGEND

- Summer
- Winter
- Year-round
- Migration

nest is securely hidden under a sapling or shrub, or in a clump of moss.

Feeding Habits

This insectivore scours leaves and flowering plants for spiders, beetles, aphids, caterpillars, flies, and grasshoppers.

Migration Habits

Highly localized populations breed throughout California north to Washington and from Minnesota across New England. Most winter in Mexico, but small groups remain along the coasts of California and Texas.

Placement of Feeders

Watch for this iridescent warbler during spring migration. Its two-part song is a high-pitched *see-it, see-it, see-it* followed by *ti-ti-ti-ti*.

yellow

Pine Siskin

yellow

I n the chilly autumn air, a flock of small, dark-colored birds undulates through the sky, alternately bunching up and fanning out. The distinctive, rising *bzzzzt* song confirms the presence of pine siskins.

Description
This 5-inch finch has a dark, streaked back, a notched tail, and small patches of yellow on the wings and tail. In flight it looks like a sparrow, but the splashes of yellow are good field markers.

Preferred Habitat
Small groups of pine siskins build their nests in conifers just a few feet apart. Here they raise two broods, then travel to mixed woodlands, alder thickets, or overgrown pastures in search of winter food.

Feeding Habits
Harvesting seeds of hemlocks, alders, birches, and cedars is the siskin's primary objective, but insects make up a small part of its diet as well.

Migration Habits
Found throughout the West year-round, some still spend winters across the eastern United States.

Placement of Feeders
Pine siskins, like other northern finches, are fond of salt and may be found along salted highways in winter. Thistle seeds are their feeder favorite, but backyard elm and ash trees can do the trick as well.

RANGE MAP

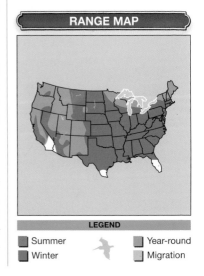

LEGEND

Summer   Year-round
Winter   Migration

In the thick silence of the deep woods, five pure notes ring out, each followed by a long pause. The eerie song of this striking bird is surprisingly simple compared to the elaborate warblings of its relatives.

Description

Adults are gray above and yellow-orange below, with light eyebrow and barred wings. Males have a broad black band across the chest. Females, with a gray or nonexistent band, are smaller than the 10-inch males.

Preferred Habitat

During migration these birds reside in parks, fields, yards, and woodland edges, but they breed in damp coniferous forests of the Pacific Northwest. The nest is a cup of twigs, plant fibers, and mud in a tall conifer.

Feeding Habits

Scattering leaf litter with its bill, the ground-forager hops back to examine the bare spot for insects, spiders, earthworms, acorns, seeds, or fruit.

Migration Habits

These thrushes live year-round along the Pacific Northwest Coast, heading north to breed. Every winter vagrants are spotted in backyards along the northern California coast.

Placement of Feeders

Birds who wander East in winter will often take up residence at a backyard feeding station for weeks or even months, where they favor berries, seeds, suet, nuts, and fruits, especially fresh oranges.

yellow

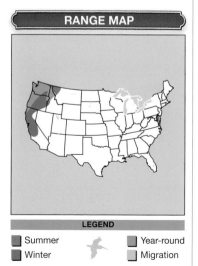

RANGE MAP

LEGEND

Summer
Winter
Year-round
Migration

Western Meadowlark

Only distinguished from the eastern meadowlark in 1844, the western bird was given the scientific name *neglecta* for being so long overlooked. The two species are nearly identical in appearance, flight, and other behaviors, but the western meadowlark confidently sings a jumble of low, clear notes, very different from its relative's song.

Description
The stocky meadowlark, 8–11 inches long, is streaked brown above, with a yellow breast marked with a black V and bright white outer tail feathers.

Preferred Habitat
In open grassland, plains, and marshes, the polygamous male constructs several dome grass nests for his mates, where each female will raise two broods a year.

In the Midwest and Southwest their range overlaps with the eastern meadowlark.

Feeding Habits
Scouring the tall grass, the bird gleans grasshoppers, crickets, beetles, cutworms, and spiders, as well as grain and seeds.

Migration Habits
In recent decades their range has spread eastward with the clearing of the forests, and they are permanent residents from Washington to central Texas, summering slightly east and north.

Placement of Feeders
When walking through their grassland habitat during nesting season, be careful not to crush their well-concealed ground nests. Watch for them perched on fence posts, utility lines, or solitary trees near open fields.

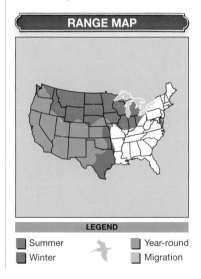

RANGE MAP

LEGEND
Summer
Winter
Year-round
Migration

A flash of bright yellow flitting into a backyard ornamental shrub may announce the presence of this 5-inch warbler, the only North American warbler to appear all yellow.

Description

Adult males are yellow-green above and bright yellow below, with two yellow tail patches and reddish stripes on the breast and belly. Juveniles and females are duller yellow to olive-green.

Preferred Habitat

A freshwater source and small trees are the ideal environment for yellow warbler colonies, commonly found in willow thickets, marshes, swamps, parks, and backyard gardens. Mating pairs construct strong nests in small trees. If parasitized by the brown-

headed cowbird, the warbler layers nest material over the unwelcome egg.

Feeding Habits

Like other warblers this species is entirely insectivorous. Males tend to search for food higher in the tree canopy than do the less conspicuous females.

Migration Habits

Traveling by night and resting by day, warbler flocks arrive in late April in the northern two-thirds of the United States. After a very short breeding season, the birds return to Mexico, and Central and South America for winter.

Placement of Feeders

The yellow warbler rarely visits feeding stations, but as flocks migrate south in late July, listen for their sweet, clear seven-note song.

RANGE MAP

LEGEND

Summer
Winter
Year-round
Migration

yellow

yellow

A s though the upper half of its body were dipped in yellow, the 9-inch yellow-head is the only North American bird with this unique coloration. Though not so common as their relatives, these marshland birds sometimes visit backyards with red-winged blackbirds.

Description
Adult males are bright yellow from the crown to breast and base of wings, and black on the tail, wings, and belly. The eye, cheeks, and chin are dark, and males have two white wing patches. Females are mostly brown, with a yellow face, white chin, and solid yellow breast.

Preferred Habitat
Loose colonies nest in cattail, bulrush, or cane marshes. Using stems of these plants, females weave a nest secured to reeds over standing water.

Feeding Habits
Plant matter, including barley, corn, and wheat crops, makes up the majority of this bird's diet, but insects such as caterpillars and grasshoppers supplement up to 40% in summer.

Migration Habits
This species breeds west of the Mississippi River into the western half of the United States. It can also be found year-round throughout the central California Valley.

Placement of Feeders
Although not a common feeder visitor, this feathered friend may be drawn to cracked corn, milo, or sunflower seeds scattered on the ground.

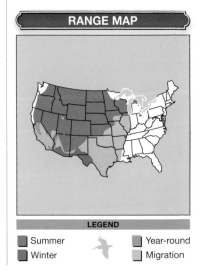

RANGE MAP

LEGEND

Summer Year-round
Winter Migration

Formerly the yellow-rump was thought to be two species, the eastern myrtle warbler and the western Audubon's warbler. The breeding males of each region look distinct, but they interbreed freely.

Description

Breeding males, 5-6 inches long, are dull blue above streaked with black, with a black breast and flanks and bright yellow on the rump, crown, and sides. Eastern males have a white throat and two white wing bars, whereas western males have a yellow throat and a large white wing patch. Females and juveniles always have the yellow rump.

Preferred Habitat

For summer breeding these warblers prefer coniferous and mixed forests, forest edges, and overgrown and cultivated

fields, where they build bulky twig nests in conifers. During other seasons they forage in a variety of habitats.

Feeding Habits

Winter populations are heavily dependent on poison ivy berries, while summer birds consume insects and berries.

Migration Habits

The widespread warbler breeds from the Pacific Northwest to New England and south to Mexico in the western half of the country. Winter finds them roosting in pine forests from their breeding range to the tropics.

Placement of Feeders

In winter these birds frequent gardens but rarely visit feeders. Listen for their frequent *chip* call to distinguish them.

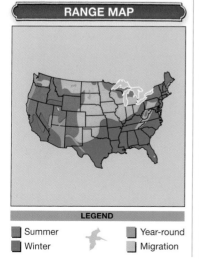

RANGE MAP

LEGEND

- Summer
- Winter
- Year-round
- Migration

yellow

Blue Jay

These brightly colored, noisy birds have a mixed reputation. Both tame and curious, they warn other birds of danger and mob predators. Yet they also eat fledglings of other species and can imitate a hawk's screech or other bird calls to claim feeders for themselves.

Description

At 12.5 inches, this large bird has an unmistakable bright blue crest, back, wings, and tail, with white tail tips, face, and underparts. Issuing a repertoire of boisterous calls, its own soft *queedle-queedle* song is seldom heard.

Preferred Habitat

Jays inhabit forests of all kinds, but oak forests are preferred. They are also common residents of gardens and parks.

Feeding Habits

One of the few birds to cache food, the jay buries seeds and acorns for winter, indirectly planting new trees. Nuts, seeds, fruits, insects, mice, and bird fledglings comprise its diet.

Migration Habits

Traveling in flocks, these birds can be found from the eastern slopes of the Great Rocky Mountains to the Atlantic Coast. Its counterpart west of the Rockies is Steller's Jay.

Placement of Feeders

These backyard bullies are frequent feeder visitors in winter, and they love sunflower seeds, suet, cracked corn, and peanuts. They are comfortable around humans, but may mob birds, squirrels, cats, or even great horned owls.

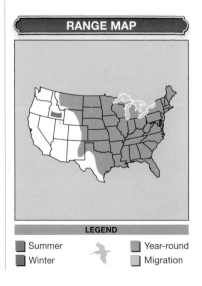

RANGE MAP

LEGEND

Summer   Year-round

Winter   Migration

blue

The incessantly active gnatcatcher cocks and flicks its long tail as it bounds through the branches. These tiny birds are fearless, readily attacking crows, jays, or other large predators who threaten their territory.

Description

Measuring 4–5.5 inches, the gnatcatcher is blue-gray above and white below with a long, black tail edged with white. Breeding males have an identifying black eyebrow, but in winter their gray eyebrow matches the female's.

Preferred Habitat

In summer the bird is at home in open mixed woodlands, especially juniper groves. Its tiny lichen-decorated nest hooked to thin twigs is often parasitized by brown-headed cowbirds. As mating pairs take turns incubating the eggs or feeding the fledglings, the male warbles incessantly at top volume.

Feeding Habits

This quick flyer can pursue fleeing insects through the treetops, hover to pick insects and spiders from leaves or flowers, or snatch tiny gnats from the air. In autumn they join mixed foraging flocks.

Migration Habits

Breeding throughout most of the United States gnatcatchers winter in select regions, one being the Desert Southwest.

Placement of Feeders

Track down this hyperactive bird by following its nasal *meehr* or buzzy *spee* call. Their high-pitched song will lead you right to their nest, which they don't attempt to conceal.

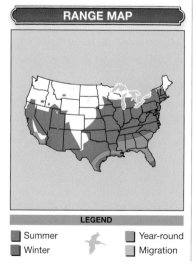

RANGE MAP

LEGEND

- Summer
- Winter
- Year-round
- Migration

blue

Mountain Bluebird

The graceful mountain bluebird is a herald of the dawn, its soft warbling song echoing off the walls of mesas and canyons as it announces the rising sun. Their song is becoming rare, though, as competition for food and habitat and changing weather patterns endanger their sensitive population.

Description
The 7-inch male is sky blue above, pale blue below, with a white belly, while the female is duller and grayer.

Preferred Habitat
Mountain bluebirds are so named for their preference for high-elevation breeding grounds, particularly meadows with scattered trees. As the temperature drops, the birds descend to grasslands and plains.

Feeding Habits
With longer wings than the eastern bluebird, this species can hover in flight, where they scan the ground for insects and berries, then drop to retrieve their meals.

Migration Habits
As the primary bluebird of the West, this species is found west of the Rockies to the northernmost regions of the lower 48 states of the U.S. It winters throughout the Desert Southwest.

Placement of Feeders
If you designate bird boxes for this delicate species, be sure to monitor them for habitation by competing cavity nesters.

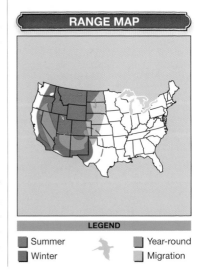

RANGE MAP

LEGEND

■ Summer
■ Winter
■ Year-round
■ Migration

blue

During spring migration, from late March to early May, the colorful male finch, giving sharp *chip* calls in flight, is a common and welcome sight.

Description
Though similar to house finches and Cassin's finches, purple finches have a bluish-purple hue. Males, 5.5–6.5 inches long, are bluish-purple above and below, fading to a pale stomach. The sparrow-like female is brown, heavily streaked below, with whitish markings on her face.

Preferred Habitat
These finches usually nest in conifers, but that may include ornamental conifers in gardens or parks. They are also found in mixed and coniferous woodlands and bottomland forests.

Feeding Habits
Finches thrive on box elder, ash, and sycamore seeds, as well as maple, birch, and aspen buds. Fruit and berries provide sustenance in winter, and insects are a treat in summer.

Migration Habits
Generally these birds breed across most of Canada, but can also be found year-round along the Pacific Coast. But when food in the northern forests is scarce, purple finches flood their southern range.

Placement of Feeders
Year after year, small groups of purple finches return to their favorite feeders, especially those featuring sunflower seeds, where these birds lend a splash of color and a rich, cheery song to the winter landscape.

RANGE MAP

LEGEND

Summer

Winter

Year-round

Migration

blue

erous forests, building their nests near the trunk of a conifer.

Feeding Habits

In summer these scavengers may supplement their diets with other songbirds' eggs, but in autumn their hoarding instincts kick in, and they busily bury acorns or other nuts in the ground for emergency winter stores.

Migration Habits

These nonmigrating residents of the great northern and western forests are found year-round from Washington to west Texas.

J ust as talented a mimic as its relatives, Steller's jay can spout a convincing hawk scream, a raucous *shaack! shaack!* shriek, or soft chattering, bubbling song. This species is the blue jay's counterpart in the West, occurring from the Rockies to the Pacific Coast.

Placement of Feeders

Shelled peanuts, nuts, seeds, and fruit are their favorite feeder foods, but they also have a tendency to raid grain fields and orchards.

Description

The largest member of the jay family, 12–13.5 inches long, is best identified by its blackish head and black-barred blue back and tail. Birds of the Northwest are darker, while southern birds have a white crescent above the eye.

Preferred Habitat

Although more reclusive than their friendly blue and gray cousins, Steller's jays may be bold and tame at campsites. They reside year-round in conif-

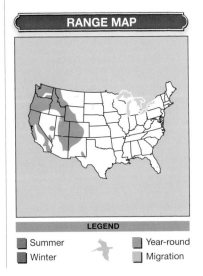

RANGE MAP

LEGEND

■ Summer   ■ Year-round
■ Winter   ■ Migration

blue

A graceful peach-necked avocet stands in shallow water, sweeping its thin upward-curving bill from side to side in search of its aquatic prey. This lovely shorebird is the world's only avocet with seasonal coloring, its head and neck changing from peachy orange in breeding season to gray in winter.

Description
Standing on long, blue-gray legs, the avocet measures up to 18 inches tall. Adults are white above with wide black stripes on the wings and back.

Preferred Habitat
American avocets may nest in loose colonies with the similar-looking black-necked stilt, seeking out salt-water or freshwater lakes, shallow ponds, beaches, marshes, mud flats, or flooded fields. Eggs are laid on the ground in a shallow depression.

Feeding Habits
With its sensitive, accurate bill the avocet catches aquatic insects as they fly past or plucks them from the water's surface. Swishing its bill underwater stirs up creatures hiding in the debris.

Migration Habits
Birders in the West eagerly await this bird's return each spring, and most colonies migrate to coastal lagoons in late autumn.

Placement of Feeders
The most noticeable field marks in flight are its long, skinny neck and boldly patterned black-and-white wings. In their aquatic habitat, you may see one swim and tip like a duck.

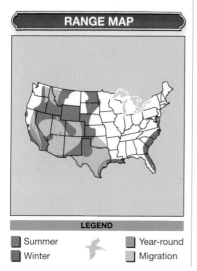

RANGE MAP

LEGEND

■ Summer   ■ Year-round
■ Winter   ■ Migration

American Redstart

An Old English word for tail is "start" and the male's bright, reddish tail, which he constantly flashes and fans, earns the name. In their Latin American wintering grounds, redstarts are known as *candelita*, or "little flame."

Description

Adult males, at about 5 inches, are glossy black with flame-colored patches on the tail, wings, and sides year-round. Females and young males are pale olive to dark gray above with bright yellow highlights and a white belly.

Preferred Habitat

Redstarts make their home in mixed and deciduous second-growth forests along swamps or streams. The season's brood is raised in a tree-bound nest of moss and grass.

Feeding Habits

Restless and active, these small birds are always in motion, scanning foliage for tiny berries, dropping to the ground to munch on seeds, then zooming away to chase an insect with the aid of bristly feathers around the beak.

Migration Habits

Wintering south of the border, the breeding ground for the American Redstart consist of most the continental United States.

Placement of Feeders

Watch for a flash of black and orange in the treetops to find these common warblers, who usually respond with interest to birders making a "pishing" or squeaking sound.

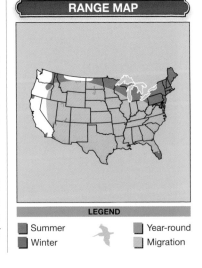

RANGE MAP

LEGEND

Summer   Year-round
Winter   Migration

black

Long ago abandoning natural nesting sites for docks, bridges, and barns, this swallow is a common sight in rural and suburban communities. Its forked tail is easily recognizable in flight, and it's the only swallow that flaps continuously, issuing a constant stream of twittering and chattering.

Description

Measuring 5-7 inches long, with a deeply forked tail and pointed wings, the barn swallow is dark blue-black above, with a red throat and pale undersides. Its flight is fast and direct, and may skim close to the ground.

Preferred Habitat

This bird favors open country or marshes near buildings and water, such as golf courses, parks, and farms.

RANGE MAP

LEGEND

- Summer
- Winter
- Year-round
- Migration

It constructs nest made of mud pellets under building eaves or on a beam.

Feeding Habits

They capture insects on the wing, and thus spend more time in flight than almost any other bird. Like other swallows, they skim the surface of rivers or lakes to drink while flying.

Migration Habits

Wintering outside the United States presents no great challenge, as the swallow travels up to 600 miles or more to reach its summer breeding grounds throughout the lower 48 states of the U.S.

Placement of Feeders

Encourage the presence of these helpful insectivores by allowing them to nest in buildings or other man-made structures.

Feeding Habits
With a sharp click of its beak, the black phoebe snatches moths, beetles, and bees from the air. Occasionally it also plucks small fish from the water's surface.

Migration Habits
This hardy flycatcher can remain in the southern part of its range over winter enjoying the year-round supply of insects. The eastern phoebe is the counterpart of this bird of the Southwest.

Placement of Feeders
A backyard pool or watering tub may satisfy the insectivorous phoebe's preference for a freshwater source, though they are commonly found near mountain streams, ponds, or rivers.

A silent, agile flyer, the black phoebe stays within a few feet of the ground, swooping from fence posts to dart after flying insects. When perched on a low tree branch, it constantly wags or dips its tail downward.

Description
The 7-inch adults are almost all black, with a white belly. Juveniles have distinct rusty wing bars.

Preferred Habitat
Phoebes are at home in a variety of environments, including marshes, ponds, streams, farmland, or canyons. Their mud and grass nest, built beneath an overhang or shelter, is extremely sturdy and durable, and home to two or three broods each season.

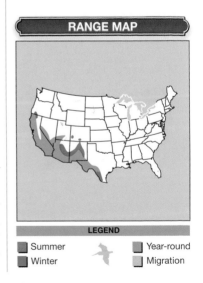

RANGE MAP

LEGEND

■ Summer		■ Year-round
■ Winter		■ Migration

black

D estruction of its marsh habitat has led to drastically reduced populations of these elegant terns. Since its appearance on the Audubon Society's Blue List of threatened species in 1971, efforts continue to preserve and protect its wetland home.

Description

This large bird, measuring 9–10.5 inches, is unmistakable in all seasons. Breeding adults are all black, with a grayish tail and white highlights on the wings. Winter birds are gray above, with a black cap, and patchy white below with white side patches.

Preferred Habitat

Alongside freshwater marshes, lagoons, and lakes, black terns build a small hollow nest on floating marsh plants. Social and gregarious, these terns usually nest and roost in colonies numbering a few to hundreds of birds.

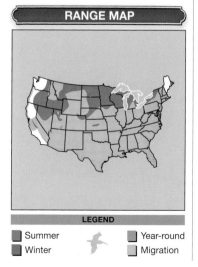

RANGE MAP

LEGEND

Summer | Year-round
Winter | Migration

Feeding Habits

This tern occasionally dives into freshwater for fish and crustaceans, but spends most of its time swooping erratically after flying insects.

Migration Habits

Their summer breeding range stretches from California to New England and north throughout Canada. In autumn they head south and seaward, wintering at sea or along the coasts of Central America and South America.

Placement of Feeders

Watch for this carnivore feeding along inland lakes and marshes. Listen for their nasal song or short *kik* call.

black

Black-billed Magpie

The notorious thievery of this striking bird was first recorded by Lewis and Clark's westward expedition in 1804. Magpies steal anything that catches their eye, from buttons and coins to food off a camper's plate, burying their treasure in the ground.

Description
Large and long-tailed at 17–22 inches long, the magpie is all black except for a bold white belly and sides.

Preferred Habitat
Magpies nest in loose colonies in farmland, prairies, open woodlands, brushy areas, or towns. Their bulky, dome-shaped twig nests are exceptionally large, measuring 2–7 feet across, and they are used year after year.

Feeding Habits
Reviled for their tendency to steal the eggs and fledglings of other birds, magpies also consume insects, fruit, and carrion.

Migration Habits
After the breeding season the birds form loose flocks of up to 20, remaining in their range of most of the interior West through southern Alaska year-round. Their close relative, the nearly identical yellow-billed Magpie, is found only in California.

Placement of Feeders
The loud, chattering calls of magpie flocks are a common sound in many neighborhoods. Watch for their huge nests, which are sometimes later occupied by foxes.

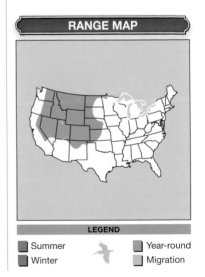

RANGE MAP

LEGEND
- Summer
- Winter
- Year-round
- Migration

In gardens and forests across North America the chickadee's acrobatic antics and sweet *chick-a-dee-dee-dee* call are familiar year-round. The chickadee is friendly and sociable, easily tamed and even hand-fed.

Description
Both sexes measure 5 inches, colored grayish above and pale below, with a bold black cap and bib, white cheeks, and white bars on black wings. In the southwest, the black-capped is replaced by the Carolina chickadee.

Preferred Habitat
Chickadees nest in tree cavities or simple bird boxes in gardens, mixed and deciduous forests, and residential areas.

Feeding Habits
Traveling in small feeding flocks, the birds work together to locate plentiful food sources, particularly in winter. They glean insects and larvae from branches and foliage, as well as seeds and berries.

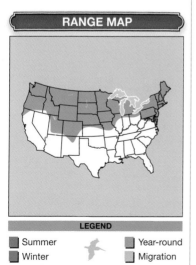

RANGE MAP

LEGEND

■ Summer
■ Winter
■ Year-round
■ Migration

Migration Habits
Across most of the northern United States from the Great Lakes to the Pacific Northwest chickadees are year-round residents. In autumn they join small mixed flocks of titmice, nuthatches, kinglets, creepers, and warblers to roost and forage together during the harsh winter months.

Placement of Feeders
Seed and suet feeders attract these cheery backyard visitors, and they are usually one of the first birds to find and inhabit a new nesting box.

visitors to flower gardens.

Feeding Habits
Nectar from flowers and small insects gleaned from foliage provide sustenance for the high-energy hummingbird.

Migration Habits
In spring, the hummingbird heads to the Southwest, where males will perform an elaborate, pendulum-like courting dance to woo their females. By summer they can be found throughout the western third of the United States. After the insect swarms of autumn end, the birds head south to Mexico.

Placement of Feeders
Like other hummingbirds, the black-chinned hummingbird is readily drawn to nectar feeders offering sugar water or nectar-rich garden flowers.

Even experts have difficulty discerning between the female black-chinned hummingbird of the West and its ruby-throated counterpart in the East. But there are discernible differences in habits; for example, black-chinned hummingbird nests, only 1.5 inches in diameter, are bound with elastic spider webs rather than lichen.

Description
The 3.75-inch male features a black chin bordered by a shiny purple band, a white collar, and dark tail; his wings make a buzzing noise in flight. The female is green above and white below.

Preferred Habitat
Found in areas as varied as oak woods, brushy fields, canyons, or orchards, these hummingbirds are also frequent

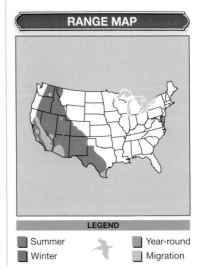

RANGE MAP

LEGEND

- Summer
- Winter
- Year-round
- Migration

As its name suggests, this heron is most active at night, but can often be seen during daylight feeding along edges of lakes and lagoons or roosting in trees. At sundown, when most herons return to the nest, these birds leave their roosts and set out to hunt.

Description

Hunched and stocky, the night heron measures 22–28 inches. Adults have a black cap and back, red eyes, gray wings, yellow legs, and a white belly. Streaky gray juveniles closely resemble the American bittern.

Preferred Habitat

In marshes, rivers, or wooded swamps, this heron piles up a mass of sticks to craft a messy platform nest. These fragile constructions are often dis-rupted by storms or high winds, dumping the chicks unceremoniously on the rubble below the rookery.

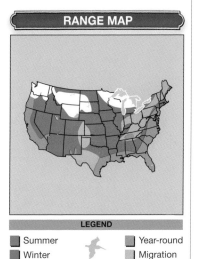

RANGE MAP

LEGEND
- Summer
- Winter
- Year-round
- Migration

Feeding Habits

Silent and menacing, the heron perches on the edge of a pond or marsh waiting for its aquatic prey—frogs, fish, and crustaceans—to chance within range.

Migration Habits

This heron summers throughout almost all states and north into central Canada, and remains year-round along the Pacific, Gulf, and Atlantic Coasts.

Placement of Feeders

Its scientific name, *nycticorax*, means "night raven." Listen for this bird's loud, barking *squawk*, a common night-time sound.

black

Black-headed Grosbeak

The black-headed grosbeak is the western counterpart of the rose-breasted grosbeak, but with more trees across the Great Plains, these two birds have begun to hybridize, casting doubt on their classification as separate species.

Description
Measuring up to 7.5 inches, males are black above, with rusty orange underparts, collar, and rump, and white patches on the wings. Females are brown above with white wing patches, a buff eyebrow, and streaked breasts.

Preferred Habitat
Unusual among birds, males incubate the eggs and sing from the nest, while females fiercely defend the nest and territory. Their flimsy twig nests are built in open, deciduous woodlands or parks near water.

Feeding Habits
Grosbeaks are named for their large, powerful, conical beaks, useful for crushing or shelling large seeds, such as those from thistles and docks, and catkins from birch and alder trees.

Migration Habits
During the summer breeding season, they are found in the western half of the United States and into British Columbia, wintering in Mexico.

Placement of Feeders
These graceful grosbeaks are welcome visitors at backyard seed feeders, where they delicately shell one sunflower seed at a time. They also consume harmful agricultural pests.

RANGE MAP

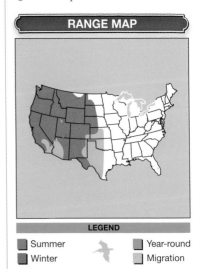

LEGEND

Summer
Winter
Year-round
Migration

black

A buzzy *zeedle-zeedle-zee* issues from a young juniper. Closer investigation reveals a cautious 5-inch warbler, its streaky black, white, and gray coloring perfectly designed for camouflage in its coniferous scrub home.

Description

Distinct in all seasons, males are solid gray above, with a black crown, bib, and cheeks. The eyebrow and "mustache" stripes are whitish, with a small yellow spot in front of each eye. Black streaks bar the white chest and belly. Females look similar, with a gray crown and a white throat.

Preferred Habitat

Look for this drab warbler flitting among juniper or pinyons in dry, deciduous or coniferous scrub forests. The durable, well-crafted nest is lined with

hair plucked from local pets or livestock, and cleverly concealed in foliage.

Feeding Habits

With the spring foliage fully unfurled, the bird forages methodically under every leaf for caterpillars, oak worms, spiders, and other small insects.

Migration Habits

This species breeds from Mexico north to British Columbia. Some remain year-round in southern California and Arizona, but most winter in northern Mexico.

Placement of Feeders

Mating pairs resort to distractions to prevent humans or would-be predators from finding the nest, but if discovered, the parents give a convincing broken-wing display.

RANGE MAP

LEGEND

■ Summer
■ Winter
■ Year-round
■ Migration

Named by John J. Audubon for the nineteenth-century ornithologist Thomas M. Brewer, this blackbird happily makes its home among humans in urban developments. As it trots along the ground, its head jerks back and forth like a chicken's.

Description

The male is solid black, up to 10 inches long, with a glossy purple-blue head. The female is dull gray with dark eyes. An excited blackbird makes an array of gurgles, squawks, and whistles, while its creaking song is *k-shee*.

Preferred Habitat

Open country, farmyards, parks, and lawns provide ample food and ideal nesting conditions. Colonies of up to 30 pairs may nest in hay fields, where the young are fledged before harvest time, or in conifers.

Feeding Habits

A year-round diet of insects and seeds is supplemented in autumn when Brewer's blackbirds swarm granaries and farms to feast on spilled grain.

Migration Habits

In summer these birds breed in small colonies, but when the fledglings can fly, they join up with neighboring colonies and flocks of red-wings, cowbirds, starlings, and grackles to form a migratory mob of tens of thousands of birds.

Placement of Feeders

Scatter seed or grain on the ground for these blackbirds to peck at.

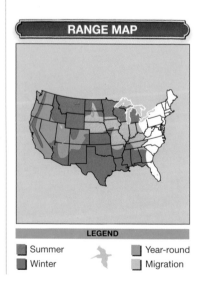

RANGE MAP

LEGEND

☐ Summer   ☐ Year-round
☐ Winter   ☐ Migration

black

Signaling the coming spring with its appearance at California's Capistrano Mission each year, the cliff swallow is known for its elaborate gourd-shaped nests, constructed out of mud on the sides of barns, buildings, or the rocky cliffs for which it is named.

Description
Distinct from the barn swallow for its square tail and pointed wings, this 6-inch swallow is blue-black on top with a white forehead and a rust-colored throat and rump.

Preferred Habitat
Open country with a fresh water source and nearby barns or buildings for nesting is the ideal environment for this bird. Unfortunately, the introduction of the house sparrow, which forces cliff swallows out of nesting sites, has reduced their population considerably.

Feeding Habits
Like other swallows, these birds snatch flying insects and airborne spiders in flight, and may dip down to drink from the surface of rivers or lakes.

Migration Habits
Widespread in North America in summer, the cliff swallow migrates southward in flocks of hundreds come autumn. They return faithfully to the same nesting sites annually, nesting in huge colonies.

Placement of Feeders
Thousands of breeding pairs have been known to nest in a single barn, but be grateful for the innumerable insects they will consume.

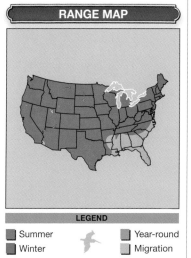

RANGE MAP

LEGEND

- Summer
- Winter
- Year-round
- Migration

black

Common Raven

For centuries this captivating black bird has earned a starring role in legends and stories around the world. In Native American myths, Irish lore, biblical tales, and modern poetry, the raven has been cast as both a sacred messenger and an ill omen.

Description
Large at 22–27 inches, the raven has long wings with feathers fanning like fingers in flight. Its wedge-shaped tail sets it apart from the American crow, and it gives a hoarse, ringing call of *crock*.

Preferred Habitat
This species favors extreme landscapes, including sea cliffs, mountains, deserts, Arctic and alpine tundra, and northern coniferous forests. Pairs mate for life, incubating their eggs in a bulky nest of sticks on a high cliff or conifer.

Feeding Habits
Scavenging ravens consume carrion, insects, crustaceans, berries, and small mammals. They compete with gulls at garbage dumps and raid seabird colonies for small birds and fledglings.

Migration Habits
Ravens are widespread nonmigrants west of the Great Plains and throughout Canada through northern Alaska, overlapping with some northern states.

Placement of Feeders
Following effective efforts to evict ravens from human communities, they are now found only in remote areas. But their sprightly aerial antics of tumbling, fighting, and diving are a show worth seeking.

RANGE MAP

LEGEND
- Summer
- Winter
- Year-round
- Migration

D ownies are the smallest and friendliest of the North American woodpeckers. Like their tree-hammering relatives, a strong bill, neck, and reinforced skull protect the brain from repeated hammering, and bristly feathers protect the nostrils.

Description

This species is a 7-inch version of the hairy woodpecker. The back and belly are white, the black wings spotted white, and the tail barred. Males have a red patch on the head, and both have a thin black mustache.

Preferred Habitat

Any urban or rural area with deciduous trees can be home to this small woodpecker. Mating pairs excavate a cavity in a tree, stump, or fence post to build the nest. Parents share incubation and feeding duties.

RANGE MAP

LEGEND

■ Summer ■ Year-round
■ Winter ■ Migration

Feeding Habits

Foraging among foliage and under bark with its sharply barbed tongue, the bird consumes insects, larvae, and grubs. In winter they can be found in weedy fields, consuming dormant wasps and corn-borers.

Migration Habits

The downy is found in almost all of North America, remaining in the North all winter to forage with chickadees and kinglets among frozen fields and backyards.

Placement of Feeders

Feeding stations featuring berries, beef suet, peanut butter, pecans, or sunflower seeds will be home to plucky downies, especially in winter.

black

European Starling

I n 1890 a Shakespeare enthusiast released 100 starlings in New York City in an effort to introduce all feathered friends mentioned in Shakespeare's works. Now numbering 200 million, starlings are noisy and messy, but they consume a large quantity of insects.

Description
Shiny black with a green or purple sheen in summer, the bird molts in autumn, growing a winter coat of white-speckled feathers. The stout, 7.5-inch starling is a skillful imitator known for its wolf-whistle call.

Preferred Habitat
Especially common around landfills or grain elevators, the starling is at home in cities, suburbs, or farmland. The female constructs a nest of twigs and trash in a tree or cavity.

Feeding Habits
City dwellers and rural residents alike can spot these birds probing for insects, spiders, worms, fruit, grain, or seeds from parks to farmyards.

Migration Habits
This native of Eurasia is found year-round from central Canada to northern Mexico. During colder months they fly in enormous swarms to roost in warmer downtown areas.

Placement of Feeders
Starlings are drawn to seed and suet feeders, but if you intend your nest boxes for native species such as bluebirds, woodpeckers, or purple martins, monitor them carefully for starling habitation.

RANGE MAP

LEGEND

■ Summer   ■ Year-round
■ Winter   ■ Migration

Great-tailed Grackle

Until the 1960s, this bird was considered the same species as its boat-tailed cousin. Where their ranges overlap, the great-tailed grackle tends to avoid salt marshes, the boat-tailed's preferred home.

Description
Almost identical in appearance to the boat-tailed bird, the great-tailed male measures 16–18 inches and is shiny black overall with an iridescent purple back. The female, 11–13 inches, is brown with a paler chest. Both have a long, keel-shaped tail and yellow eyes (compared to the brownish eyes of the boat-tailed).

Preferred Habitat
Grackles prefer open country near water, including farmlands with scattered trees or thickets. They nest in loose colonies, and may nest in mixed colonies with boat-tailed birds, but rarely interbreed.

RANGE MAP

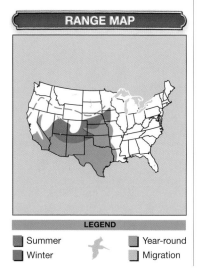

LEGEND
- Summer
- Winter
- Year-round
- Migration

Feeding Habits
From their waterside roosts, grackles prey on small fish, aquatic creatures, insects, and other birds' eggs and fledglings.

Migration Habits
This grackle is found in California, Colorado, and western Louisiana southward. Experts surmise that the species is extending its range east, but it hasn't yet reached Florida.

Placement of Feeders
If you encounter one, distinguish the great-tailed grackle from the boat-tailed species by listening to its song, a variety of loud, piercing whistles, clucks, high-pitched squealing, and hissing. The boat-tailed has a lower-toned, rolling song.

black

Hairy Woodpecker

Woodpeckers are not known for vocalization, and despite their sharp *peek* call, the birds prefer to regale each other with a drumming "song" made by jackhammering dead tree trunks with their stout bills.

Description

Larger than the similar downy woodpecker, the 9-inch hairy species is mainly black above, with white-spotted wings and a white back, and white below. The head has a black crown, stripes on the face, and small red patches. Juveniles are brown.

Preferred Habitat

This shy forest bird is found in mixed and coniferous forests, wooded swamps, and river bottoms. In the spring parent birds busily excavate a cavity in a tree or shrub to house their eggs.

Feeding Habits

Using its sturdy tail like a tripod, this woodpecker hammers into tree trunks and shreds strips of bark to excavate wood-boring insects, bark beetles, ants, and spiders, or the occasional hazelnut or acorn.

Migration Habits

Regardless of the season or weather conditions, this bird can be found in all states, cheerily chipping away loose tree bark.

Placement of Feeders

The hairy woodpecker is not so common a backyard visitor as the downy, but it is drawn to raw apples, bananas, peanut butter, and sunflower seeds, and it is especially fond of beef suet.

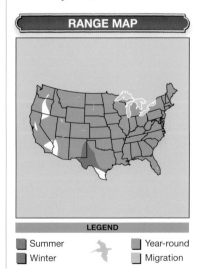

RANGE MAP

LEGEND

Summer
Winter
Year-round
Migration

This species was formerly grouped with the eastern towhee as the rufous-sided towhee because they hybridize on the Great Plains; it also hybridizes with the collared towhee in Mexico. The spotted is nearly identical to the eastern, but the latter lacks the white wing bars and back spots.

Description

Medium-sized at 8.5 inches, the red-eyed male is black above with a white belly, while females are paler brownish. The wings and back are spotted white with two white wing bars, and the sides and flanks are rusty.

Preferred Habitat

In summer spotted towhees are common in scrubby, brushy areas and overgrown fields, where they build a nest of bark, dead leaves, and plant matter on or near the ground.

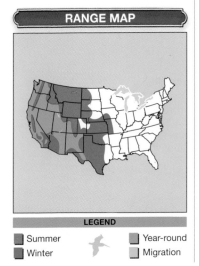

Feeding Habits

The towhee uses two-footed "double scratching" to search the ground for seeds, insects, caterpillars, ants, beetles, acorns, and fruits.

Migration Habits

This species is common and abundant, breeding from the Pacific Coast east to Texas and into Mexico, and wintering from southern Idaho to Colorado and Kansas.

Placement of Feeders

The trilling song of the towhee announces its arrival at backyard feeding stations, where it demonstrates its characteristic backward hopping on the ground beneath seed feeders.

American Pipit

Tiny but hardy, the pipit nests only in the harsh tundra environment. American birders are likely to see them during migration, where they rest in mud flats and wet grain fields, though nesting pairs do appear throughout the Rocky Mountain range.

Description

Breeding birds, at 5–7 inches long, are grayish above and buff below with a white-rimmed tail. Autumn birds are streaky gray-brown above and heavily streaked white below. The thin legs and beak are dark.

Preferred Habitat

Males establish nesting territories on alpine or Arctic tundra before the snow melts, ready for a quick breeding season. During nonbreeding season they can be found on dunes, plowed fields, and shores.

Feeding Habits

Walking slowly on sturdy legs, the pipit consumes insects, spiders, snails, mayflies, and dragonflies and their larvae. In winter it eats mainly seeds.

Migration Habits

In March males head to their breeding range in the Rocky Mountains north to Alaska and the Arctic Circle, while females follow in May. In September, flocks head south to the southern United States and Central and South America.

Placement of Feeders

The pipit seldom stops to perch, but listen for its quick *pipit* call in flight and observe its constant tail-bobbing action.

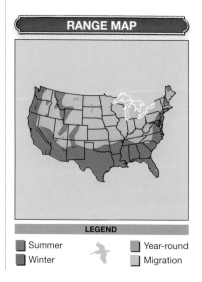

RANGE MAP

LEGEND

- Summer
- Winter
- Year-round
- Migration

gray

As the herald of spring in northern states, the robin's chipper call of *cheerily cheer up cheerio* pierces the early morning stillness. Although technically a thrush—and the only widespread thrush in America—the bird is named for its resemblance to the red-breasted robin of Europe.

Description
The male, at 9–11 inches long, is gray on top, with a black head and bright red breast. The female is similar in appearance but duller, with a gray head.

Preferred Habitat
Lawns, gardens, parks, forests, and farmland are favorite locations, but birds that winter in the northern states may roost in cedar bogs and swamps.

RANGE MAP

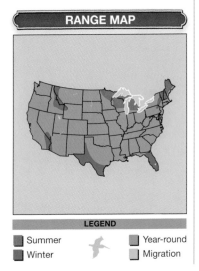

LEGEND
- Summer
- Winter
- Year-round
- Migration

Feeding Habits
As it hops across a lawn with its head cocked, the robin is hunting for insects and earthworms. Berries provide sustenance through the winter.

Migration Habits
Though not all robins head south for the winter, each year huge flocks of up to 300,000 birds head northward in spring, with each bird returning to the area of his birth.

Placement of Feeders
While not regular visitors to feeders, they may be drawn to mealworms, bread, raisins, or fruit. They are easily sighted on a grassy lawn rooting for worms, and may build nests on ledges or windowsills.

gray

Barn Owl

Piercing the night with a spine-tingling hiss and scream, the barn owl pursues an evening meal of mice or rabbits. This owl species is tolerant of human presence, often making its home in barns.

Description
The barn owl, at 13-19 inches long, is easily recognized by its long legs, dark eyes, and heart-shaped face. Colored golden brown with a greyish hue above and white below, it appears pure white in flight.

Preferred Habitat
A widespread species, the barn owl is found on six of seven continents, where it inhabits grasslands, marshes, deserts, and residential and urban areas.

Feeding Habits
Garbage dumps, cemeteries, and farms are favorite hunting grounds for rodents, small mammals, or other birds. The owl has good daytime eye-sight, but can track its prey by sound alone in complete darkness.

Migration Habits
The barn owl inhabits almost all states year-round, laying eggs in buildings, hollow trees, caves, or burrows. They also practice population control, producing few or no eggs when food is scarce.

Placement of Feeders
These nocturnal hunters can be seen soaring alongside highways or rural roads at dusk as they scan the ground for prey, and they may select a local barn or bell tower for nesting.

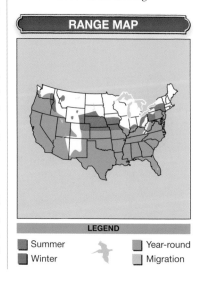

RANGE MAP

LEGEND

Summer   Year-round
Winter   Migration

gray

A long a quiet river bank, a large blue-gray bird with a ragged crest issues a rattling *crick-crick-crick* from a nearby perch. The kingfisher is an aggressive, independent hunter.

Description
Pigeon-sized at 11–14 inches long, this crested bird is blue-gray above with a crest and white collar. The male has a blue-gray band across the chest, while the female has two chest bands and brighter coloring.

Preferred Habitat
These fish-eaters never stray far from water. The mating pair tunnels into the bank alongside a favorite river or lake, where the female lays eggs in the cool, dark burrow.

Feeding Habits
Hovering over the water, a flash of blue spirals into a deadly dive, clutching a stunned fish back to its perch, where it beats the fish and swallows it whole. Bones and scales are later regurgitated as pellets. Favorite foods include fish, tadpoles, salamanders, frogs, insects, crabs, or crayfish. Young are taught to retrieve dead fish from the water.

Migration Habits
Found year-round throughout most of the West, this fierce fisher travels to northern border states during summer only.

Placement of Feeders
Patient observation along the water's edge will reveal favorite perches and may allow you to witness their diving spectacle.

RANGE MAP

LEGEND
- Summer
- Winter
- Year-round
- Migration

gray

Bushtit

Tiny and long-tailed, the pert bushtit is a treetop acrobat, often seen swiveling on leaves, swinging upside down, and spinning around in frenetic foraging antics. They are one of the few species to have a "helper" assist the mating pair in raising their chicks.

Description

Plain and dark, the bushtit measures 4.5 inches, with a gray or brown cap. Males have dark eyes and females have pale eyes. A black-cheeked race occurs in parts of Texas and Arizona.

Preferred Habitat

Flocks of 10 to 40 birds are common residents in open pine or oak woodlands, suburban parks, and gardens. The gourd-shaped nest is a hanging pouch at least 10 inches long.

Feeding Habits

Swinging upside down like the chickadee, the bushtit plucks insects, aphids, and spiders from the undersides of foliage. The entire flock feeds in a single tree, then moves en masse to the next foraging area.

Migration Habits

During breeding season, bushtits travel and nest in small flocks, joining larger foraging groups in autumn. They are found year-round in the West from Washington to Texas.

Placement of Feeders

Listen for a rapid, constant, high-pitched twittering. Making a quick *squeak* noise can lure them quite close, for they are not intimidated by humans.

RANGE MAP

LEGEND

■ Summer   ■ Year-round
■ Winter   ■ Migration

gray

Once known as the "chicken hawk" for its preference for barnyard fowl, this large hawk was hunted by the thousands, and many other hawk species suffered the same fate. Populations also diminished temporarily with the use of DDT.

Description
This species is almost identical to the sharp-shinned hawk, but larger and more powerful at 15–20 inches long. Adults are dark blue-gray above and white-barred red below, with a dark cap. Juveniles are streaked with brown.

Preferred Habitat
Open deciduous forests and mixed woodlands are traditional habitats of Cooper's hawks, but they are increasingly common in urban and suburban yards. In their high platform nest of

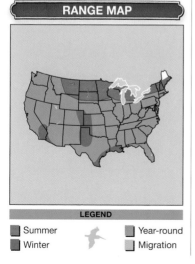

RANGE MAP

LEGEND

- Summer
- Winter
- Year-round
- Migration

sticks, the male feeds the incubating female, and she feeds the chicks.

Feeding Habits
The large hawk is easily outmaneuvered by songbirds, but it relies on surprise and speed to catch birds, squirrels, and chipmunks. It may return with its captured meal to a feeding roost.

Migration Habits
The species is found year-round in almost all states except the Great Plains, breeding slightly north into southern Canada and wintering in the lower majority of its range.

Placement of Feeders
These woodland birds are best identified as they glide overhead by their rounded wings and long, rounded tail.

gray

This fierce-looking bird of the desert makes its home right in the center of a spiny cholla cactus, where the formidable spikes provide a safe haven from hawks, snakes, or other would-be predators.

Description
Long and slender at 10–12 inches, adult thrashers are pale grayish brown above and spotted below. Their long tails are rimmed with white. Note their striking yellow or orange eyes and the downward-curving black bill.

Preferred Habitat
These thrashers are found in deserts with brush or cholla cactus, thickets, dry farmland, and nearby gardens. The mating pair takes turns incubating the eggs in their nest of thorny twigs built within a cactus or thorny shrub.

Feeding Habits
Using its curved bill the bird scatters leaves and plant debris or digs holes in the soil in search of insects, seeds, berries, fruits, spiders, and small reptiles.

Migration Habits
Thriving in many habitats, the curve-billed is the most widespread western thrasher. It is found year-round in the deserts of the Southwest, from Arizona to Colorado into Texas and Mexico.

Placement of Feeders
Although its loud, whistled *whit-wheet* is a familiar sound in the desert brush, the bird prefers to forage quietly. It will visit gardens for raw apples or rolled oats.

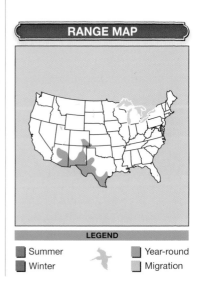

RANGE MAP

LEGEND

■ Summer	■ Year-round
■ Winter	■ Migration

gray

The dark-eyed species consolidates what were formerly thought to be up to five different species: the slate-colored, Oregon, white-winged, pink-sided, and gray-headed juncos. But despite their varied coloring, these birds breed freely with each other, and all issue a similar, slow, musical trill.

Description

All measuring 5–6.5 inches long, with a pinkish bill and dark eyes, there are distinct plumage variations. The eastern slate bird is gray above and below; the gray-head of the southern Rockies is rust or brown above; the pink-sided junco of the Central Rockies has pinkish marks on its sides; the Oregon variety has a black head and brown back, while the white-winged version of the Black Hills has white wing bars and tail.

Preferred Habitat

Juncos live in open woodlands and clearings throughout North America.

Feeding Habits

With a unique double-scratching motion, juncos dig for insects. They also enjoy seeds and berries.

Migration Habits

Found throughout the continental United States in the winter. It can be found year-round throughout the western third of the United States.

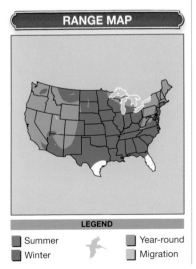

RANGE MAP

LEGEND

Summer

Winter

Year-round

Migration

Placement of Feeders

One of the most frequent feeder visitors in winter, juncos prefer millet, sunflower hearts, and finely cracked corn from low platform feeders.

gray

When the female leaves the nest, she plugs it with a loose cap of fur.

Feeding Habits

Hanging upside down, the chickadee plucks insects, seeds, and berries from foliage. Like other chickadees, this bird sometimes stashes seeds in a tree cavity or in the ground for later use.

Migration Habits

Small flocks are found year-round in the West, from British Columbia south through the Cascade and Rocky Mountain ranges to California and western Texas. These nonmigrants tend to claim a small territory for life.

Investigating a cheery, whistled *fee-bee-bay* or *chicka-dee-dee* will lead you to this high-elevation chickadee, only distinguished from its black-capped and Carolina cousins by a white eyebrow in its black cap.

Placement of Feeders

Within their range, these chickadees readily frequent seed feeders and nesting boxes.

Description

The 5.5-inch chickadee is gray above and buff below, with a black cap and bib, white eyebrow and cheeks, and gray sides. Its bill, feet, and legs are also black.

Preferred Habitat

This species makes its home in dry coniferous, ponderosa, or aspen forests in mountainous areas, as well as juniper groves in winter. The cavity nest of plant fibers and mammal fur is built in a tree cavity or birdhouse.

gray

RANGE MAP

LEGEND

Summer   Year-round
Winter   Migration

Northern Mockingbird

From dawn to dusk and sometimes all through the night, the northern mockingbird croons a steady, rapid stream of hundreds of bird songs, interspersed with occasional barking dog and chirping cricket imitations. Its Latin name means "mimic of many tongues."

Description
This slender, gray bird measures 9–11 inches, with a long black tail bordered by white that it flicks from side to side. Both sexes flash their two white wing bars and large white side patches.

Preferred Habitat
Fiercely territorial, mockingbirds will attack crows and grackles, and even cats during breeding season. They will also attack their own reflections with enough violence to cause injury or occasionally death. In lawns, gardens, farmland, or deserts, they live on the ground, hiding in bushes as needed, but mounting a high perch to sing.

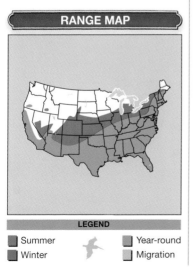

RANGE MAP

LEGEND

Summer   Year-round

Winter   Migration

Feeding Habits
This ground feeder forages in foliage and short grass for insects, grasshoppers, spiders, and fruit.

Migration Habits
Found year-round from California to Texas to New England, mockingbirds may migrate north in summer.

Placement of Feeders
Mockingbirds are heard singing at night more than other birds in their family, and can be identified in flight by their white wing patches and extremely slow wing beats. Suet and raisins are favorites at the feeder.

gray

Oak Titmouse

F ormerly known as the plain titmouse, this 5-inch creature has a
high-pitched, whistled song, but
usually feeds and forages quietly.

Description

Unremarkable adults are plain gray
above and paler below, with a small
gray head crest. This species is nearly
identical to the juniper titmouse, with
which it was grouped as the plain species, but their ranges overlap only in
parts of California.

Preferred Habitat

In their first breeding season these titmice form lifelong mating pairs, defending their preferred territories year-round.
In parks or forests of oak, pine, pinyon,
or juniper, the birds seek natural cavities
for roosting and nesting.

Feeding Habits

Pert and acrobatic, the oak titmouse
hangs upside down to glean insects,
poison oak seeds, and berries. During
nesting season, parent birds also collect
grubs, caterpillars, and pupae to carry
back to their hungry chicks.

Migration Habits

A year-round resident in the West, the
bird's range stretches from southern
Oregon south to California.

Placement of Feeders

Unlike others of its kind, this titmouse
does not travel in mixed flocks and is
usually spotted foraging alone. Fortu-
nately for backyard birders, the species readily visits seed feeders and uses
nest boxes.

RANGE MAP

LEGEND

■ Summer ■ Year-round
■ Winter ■ Migration

gray

This favorite among bird enthusiasts sports a thick plumage of mottled feathers. This is the western equivalent of the well-known eastern screech owl. This night-time hunter glides silently through the oaks and pines of western forests to snatch its prey.

Description
Identified by its distinctive ear tufts, fixed yellow eyes, and white wing spots, the 10-inch gray or red owl gives a variety of chilling calls, including screeching, purring, trilling, and a descending wail.

Preferred Habitat
The western species prefers mature oak forests, and mixed woods. They tend to be found nesting in an available recess in a tree.

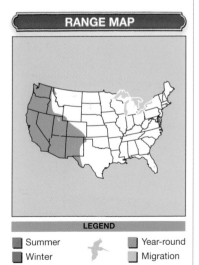

RANGE MAP

LEGEND

■ Summer   ■ Year-round
■ Winter   ■ Migration

Feeding Habits
Hunting at night on silent wings, the owl scoops up rodents, birds, earthworms, and snakes with its deadly talons. It can also catch insects on the wing or plunge into streams to snatch fish.

Migration Habits
The western screech owl is a year-round resident west of the Rockies. They remain established where they nest and thrive.

Placement of Feeders
Birders may never detect the owl's nighttime visits to backyard birdbaths, but the elusive guest sometimes uses nest boxes. Listen for their loud horse-whinny calls after dark.

gray

Feeding Habits

Using its long, thin bill, the nuthatch forages under loose bark and in tree crevices for insects and larvae.

Migration Habits

Nuthatches are found year-round in almost all continental states. Occasionally they migrate to the outer coasts in winter but are usually sedentary. In winter nuthatches join flocks of chickadees, woodpeckers, and kinglets to roam for food within their territories.

Placement of Feeders

Seed feeders and suet cakes draw these familiar winter visitors to backyard feeders. They are cheery and friendly, though not tame, and will use available nest boxes.

A n extra long hind toe claw allows the nuthatch to creep down tree trunks headfirst. Like its red-breasted relative, the white-breasted nuthatch gives a low-pitched *yank-yank* call and a low whistled song, including a *whi-whi-whi-whi* mating song.

Description

Larger than the red-breast, this bird measures 5–6 inches, colored blue-gray above with a black crown and white underparts. Its black eye is conspicuous in a white face.

Preferred Habitat

Mating pairs remain together year-round, usually in dry oak or pine oak forests or other deciduous forests. Adult birds nest in a natural cavity or bird box, or excavate a new hole.

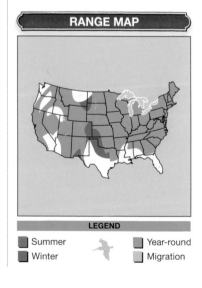

RANGE MAP

LEGEND

Summer   Year-round

Winter   Migration

white

The white-breasted rufous hummingbird is noteworthy as the hummingbird with the most extensive migration in North America. As with all hummingbirds, the in-flight manueverability and feeding habits of this species is a marvel to see.

Description
This species is easily identified by the white breast and rufous coloring. The male has a rufous body, while the female is green. Both are stocky, only 3-4 inches long.

Preferred Habitat
Look for these flashy birds in shrubbery, open woods, and along the Pacific Coast. It is likely you will see them over and over, as they are creatures of habit and return to feeding stations year after year.

Feeding Habits
Using its long, needle-like beak, the hummingbird extracts nectar and small insects from flowers in western meadows.

Migration Habits
Unusual among hummingbirds, the rufous spends its summers in the Northwest and utilizes the West for its migration. From western Texas to the Pacific Coast, this species is the most migratory of them all.

Placement of Feeders
Tubular red flowers and honeysuckle around your property are likely to attract the rufous. Since hummingbirds must constantly feed, you will spot them hovering and feeding in your western backyard.

RANGE MAP

LEGEND

- Summer
- Winter
- Year-round
- Migration

white

Feeding Habits

Scratching the ground with its large toes, the bird reveals insects, seeds, and grain, but also captures insects on the wing. When available, it eats wild fruits and buds.

Migration Habits

This partial migrant breeds from California to Colorado north to Alaska and across Canada, wintering in the southern half of the United States.

Placement of Feeders

Detailed studies have been done on these perky, friendly sparrows. Huge flocks visit winter feeders for apples, pecans, millet, peanuts, or sunflower seeds. Listen for their *chink* call, and capture their interest with any squeaking noise.

Easily identified by its distinctive head markings, the white-crowned is one of few sparrows to sing year-round, caroling its bright melodies through snowy winter days. Their songs are learned locally, so many "dialects" occur.

Description

This large sparrow, up to 7.5 inches long, is named for its black-and-white striped crown (juveniles have brown-and-tan stripes). Adults are streaky brown above and plain gray below, with a gray face and white throat.

Preferred Habitat

These sparrows summer in spruce forest, brushy thickets, bogs, meadows, and lawns, wintering in open woods and gardens. Their nest is a bulky cup of grass and twigs on the ground or in a tree.

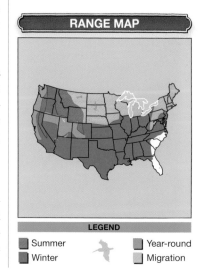

RANGE MAP

LEGEND

☐ Summer ☐ Year-round

☐ Winter ☐ Migration

white

Among white-throated sparrows, two coloring variations occur—white head stripes or tan head stripes—and birds tend to choose mating pairs with the opposite coloring. Their clear, whistled song has been transcribed in several ways, but *sweet, sweet Canada, Canada, Canada* is a common translation.

Description

The sexes look the same, measuring 6–7 inches long, streaked brown above and buff or gray below. Both have a conspicuous white throat patch, a dark bill, and yellow patches between the eyes.

Preferred Habitat

Brushy undergrowth in coniferous forests is the sparrow's preferred breeding ground, where it builds a nest of grass and moss on or near the ground under small trees. In winter, they are found in brushy areas, pastures, bogs, and suburbs.

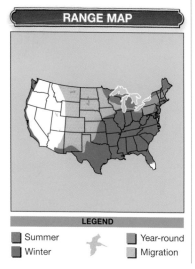

RANGE MAP

LEGEND

■ Summer
■ Winter
■ Year-round
■ Migration

Feeding Habits

The sparrow captures insects by scratching on the ground, scouring vegetation, or flycatching. Weed seeds and the fruit of dogwood, sumac, and elderberry trees are also favorites.

Migration Habits

Best known in the United States as a winter visitor, they reside across most of the East and along the West Coast, with a breeding range in the North.

Placement of Feeders

In cold months, backyard bushes may be filled with roosting white-throats. They are drawn to feeders offering cracked corn or seeds.

white

On a scorching hot summer day, a drawn out *hooo-hooo-ho-hooo* flows constantly from the perched dove. When startled, the dove flares from the roost flashing its bright white wing patches, clapping straight up, then soaring gracefully back down.

Description
The large, 12-inch dove is gray-brown above, and its black wings are marked with a broad white diagonal bar. In flight its white-edged rounded tail is most noticeable.

Preferred Habitat
Huge colonies of white-winged doves nest together, building fragile twig platforms in low bushes. Their preferred home is open country with dense thickets or small trees, farmland, or residential areas, but in summer they are often found in southern deserts alongside streams.

Feeding Habits
This dove relies on cultivated fields for sorghum and other crop grains. They may travel long distances each day to reach the nearest freshwater source.

Migration Habits
Since being introduced in southern Florida, several localized populations occur along the Gulf Coast to southern Texas. In winter, they head further south to Central and South America and the American tropics.

Placement of Feeders
Watch for the white wing bands and white-tipped tail to identify this bird in the field. Cracked corn under backyard feeders may draw them into closer view.

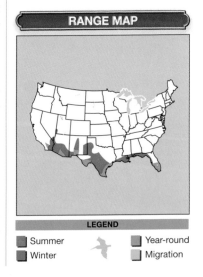

RANGE MAP

LEGEND

| Summer | Year-round |
| Winter | Migration |

white

INDEX

INDEX